Touched by Untouchables

My Life and work in India

Pat Atkinson

Connaught Books

First published in Great Britain in 2012 by Connaught Books

The right of Pat Atkinson to be identified as author of this work has been asserted by her in accordance with the copyright, Designs and Patents Act 1988

British Library Cataloguing in Publication Data

A catalogue record for this book is available from the British Library

ISBN 978-0-9557454-2-3

Printed in England by the Lavenham Press Ltd.

Every effort has been made to contact copyright holders and obtain relevant permissions.

A Connaught Books Publication

For Brian, Jo and Claire

The real heroes…………

Contents

Acknowledgements   1
Foreword   3
Prologue   5
Chapter 1   My First Trip to India   9
Chapter 2   Early Dreams of India   19
Chapter 3   From Bingo Caller to Deaconess   27
Chapter 4   The Work Begins: Meeting the Children   33
Chapter 5   The School for Disabled Children   41
Chapter 6   A New Level of Commitment   45
Chapter 7   Children of the Streets   49
Chapter 8   Entering the Slum   57
Chapter 9   The Frail and the Sick   63
Chapter 10   A Serious Illness: I Nearly Give Up   75
Chapter 11   The Work Expands   81
Chapter 12   Jacob and the Trivandrum Boys' and Girls' Homes   83
Chapter 13   Trips Away   85
Chapter 14   Train Journeys and Meeting Mother Teresa   89
Chapter 15   Exploited Hotel Workers   95
Chapter 16   A Child of the Gutter   101
Chapter 17   A New Children's Centre in Madurai   105
Chapter 18   Focusing on the Special Needs of Girls and Women   109
Chapter 19   Working in Medical Centres   115
Chapter 20   The Tsunami Creates New Needs   119
Chapter 21   Extending the Work to Sri Lanka   125
Chapter 22   A New Beginning in Mavelikara   131
Chapter 23   Return to Madurai: Muthukumar Joins the Team   139
Chapter 24   Where we are Now and Some Thoughts about the Future 147
Chapter 25   Reflections on my Work and my Faith   153
Epilogue   159

Acknowledgements

That this book exists at all is down to three people. First, I am deeply indebted to the wonderful writer, Brian Vincent. It was he who sat for hundreds of hours over several years taping my stories, reflections and memories. He quickly saw what I was trying to say and organised pages and pages of material into a coherent narrative which he placed between a thought-provoking prologue and epilogue. Brian's work provides the backbone to this book.

I am also very indebted to Carole and Michael Blackwell, both published authors and experienced editors. They were very willing to work with the book to ensure that Brian's initial work could indeed reach publication. Here again I met commitment, dedication and countless hours of work to restructure the original writing to include later developments and to prepare it for commercial publication. The Trust is extremely grateful to the three of them; they know that any profits made from the book will aid its future work.

I am very grateful to Joyce Collins, Dinah Harrison, Malory Makower, and Judith Elsey who read my manuscript and made most helpful comments. I also want to thank my friends in Brundall who read and commented on the manuscript: Jean and Arthur, David and Barbara, Shirley and George, John and Barbara, and Maureen and Ian. Over the years, they have been a much valued support group for me. During my visits to India they often meet up to pray for me.

However, there would have been no story to write without our loyal supporters through the years. Their financial, prayerful and consistent support have enabled me to fulfil what I am certain is my vocation in life and, most of all, have transformed the lives of hundreds of those who thought that no-one cared for them or about them. Through good times and bad their loyalty and commitment have been my strength and driving force. I struggle every time I write a report to say an adequate "thank you" because I am the one privileged to see the results of their giving: maybe this book will explain more.

1

The real heroes are my wonderful family. None of us planned the events that happened: the story began with what we assumed would be a one-off trip. We then thought the second trip (when I was accompanied by 14 year old Claire), would be the final one, but of course they continued. To be honest I have had to face a fair bit of criticism about leaving them for weeks at a time – "What about your husband and family" has been said to me on many occasions. I have to acknowledge that the work did make an impact on our family finances, particularly when I took myself out of pension schemes and regular work for several years, but my family never objected. We have always been extremely close. The encouragement from Brian, Jo and Claire has never faltered and their support has always been absolute. Jo, who has been to India five times (at her own expense), has seen for herself how lives are being transformed and has returned home to share her excitement about the work with Brian and Claire. In a strange way the separations (and reunions) have probably made us even stronger as a unit. The role of my family and the support they have given me is a sign of the love we share.

Foreword

There are no two ways about it. This is a fascinating book—informative and intelligently written but deeply moving too. What makes it so is the fact that for more than two decades Pat has been spending several weeks a year inside some of India's very worst slums. Not driving past them and taking a few quick photos—but walking through them and sitting for hours on end talking to sick and dying people in their tumbledown shacks or their spot on the pavement. And then, for several of the earlier years, returning at night to the very basic non-air conditioned lodgings she shared with cockroaches and mosquitoes. She tells her story in a way that makes you feel the heat and humidity, smell the cooking fires and open sewers, and hear the tales told by exuberant youngsters and, more haltingly, by elderly grandmas. It is a remarkably insightful story.

Michael writes: I have to confess that I approached this book with some trepidation. I spent my career working in overseas development and like most members of my profession have an inbuilt prejudice against the 'amateur'. Shame on me—I wasn't far into the book before I realised how perceptively Pat had analysed the social structures of poverty and the relationship between short-term palliative measures and long-term social change. I was also a bit wary knowing that Pat was an ordained minister of the Church. I often find that accounts of Christian service in poor countries are permeated by a theology that I don't really share and by a rather heavy dose of sentimentality. This is not at all the case for Pat's book. She makes clear that it was her religion that sensitised her to the suffering of poor people and imbued her with a sense of mission to do something about it—but she never preaches. Most of the book is a vivid and practical account of her life among the untouchables of Kerala and Tamil Nadu and it is only at the end of the book that she discusses in detail the relationship between her work and her faith. I found these reflections very thought-provoking.

Carole writes: When Mother Teresa was approaching the end of her life, Pat was one of the few people she allowed into her room to visit her. The elderly nun, then very frail, squeezed Pat's hand, commended her work and said: "Don't stop loving. Don't stop loving". And she hasn't. Pat's love for the people she works with is apparent to anyone who hears her speak, and when I accompanied her on her 41st visit to India, I was able to see this love in action: the smiles of the frail little grannies as our auto rickshaw pulled up outside the home; the lady who said, "No one has ever cared for me before"; the bright eyed children who couldn't wait to tell us about the concert they were presenting in the slum community hall; the lady with advanced leprosy who shuffled to the drop-in centre on her bottom. (She now has a wheelchair and is receiving medical treatment.) So many lives transformed because a Norfolk lady cared.

During my visit I got to know Muthukumar and Jacob who now head the main projects, and the dedicated staff and volunteers who work with them. I also saw some of the long-term effects of Pat's work. 'Slumdogs' she befriended are graduating from university and going on to play their part in India's impressive economic revival. Many are giving hours of their time to help the children currently attending the projects. Were it not for Pat, her colleagues and her donors, these men and women would probably still be in the slums employed, if at all, in the most menial and dirty jobs.

This is one of those rare books that changes the way we think for ever. It helps us see some of the world's poorest people not merely as an amorphous group but as individuals who have the same hopes, fears and aspirations as we do. It is a wonderful example of how an 'ordinary person' (as Pat calls herself) can act with extraordinary courage and self-sacrifice and make a lasting impact for good in the lives of people who are lower than those at the very bottom of the caste system.

Prologue

The boy crouched in the shadow of the rough timber shack, his legs hunched up and his head drooped towards his knees as though he were asleep. It was early afternoon. All was quiet in the Indian village that stretched alongside National Highway 47. Everything—the road, the shacks, the trees—was the same shade of sandy brown, burnt from the intense heat of the sun. Occasionally, a truck passing through broke the stillness and left in its wake a choking cloud of dust. Here and there, one or two women moved lazily between the shacks. A stray mangy dog stopped near the boy to drink from the open sewer drain that ran along the edge of the road. Neither the dog nor the women took any notice of the boy. As far as they were concerned he didn't exist.

The boy had a name but it didn't matter. He was no more than the dust of the earth. He was fourteen, maybe fifteen years old, and he was dying. His life was hopeless but it had been hopeless from the day he was born. He was a Dalit, an untouchable, the lowest of the low, excluded from the caste system of India and regarded as almost less than human. He felt no bitterness for it never occurred to him that he was entitled to anything more. The gods had predestined his fate. His karma was to suffer. Not for him the promise that, with each successive reincarnation after death, he might be reborn into a better existence. No, his lot was to remain forever a Dalit, an outcast.

He never knew his father and he could only vaguely remember his mother. She might have been a rag-picker, a stonebreaker, or a prostitute. He remembered little of his early life: of growing up in the slums, of working almost as soon as he could walk, of paddling in the open sewers looking for waste to salvage. He did not think his childhood unusual, for in the slums where he lived there were thousands like him. As he grew older, he found himself begging on the streets, a prey to sexual predators. Now he was weak and ill and no longer of interest to them. His once appealing boyish face was scabbed and dried as parched paper. Flecks of dried blood stained the corners of his mouth. He seemed unaware of the flies that crawled across the open weeping sores that disfigured his body. His eyes, deep in their sockets, showed that death was beckoning.

His head lifted as he heard the sound of a vehicle. It was quieter than a truck and his interest was aroused. He squinted into the distance and saw a minibus. He sat not moving as the vehicle approached. It slowed as it drew near, passing by to pull into the side of the road. The swirling dust made him cough and a dribble of fresh blood seeped from the corner of his mouth.

The sliding doors clanged open and out poured a group of foreign tourists. The Indian driver disappeared into the local drinks station and re-emerged with bottled drinks. The boy stirred. In the city, frightened tourists shied away from him repelled by his appearance but in this quiet backwater it was possible one of the foreigners would give him money or food if he made the effort. As he struggled to stand, he coughed again and spat out a globule of sputum and blood. He leant hard on a stick and as his body uncurled, his skin stretched tightly over his skeletal frame. It was hard to see how his bent spindly legs were able support his swollen belly. Leprosy had eaten away most of one hand but he needed both to hold on to his stick. His clothes, such as they were, clung to him in shreds and barely covered his body.

The foreigners were laughing and drinking. He moved towards them in jerky awkward movements pushing the stick in front of him for support as he hobbled along. He moved slowly so as not to startle them by his approach. From the banter that passed between them he recognised they were English. As he neared them, a woman in the group, standing slightly apart from the rest, turned and caught his eye. She wore a t-shirt and pale cotton skirt that hung loosely about her, so different from the bright-patterned saris he was used to seeing.

He walked awkwardly towards her and stopped. She didn't recoil but instead took a step closer to him. She reached out and touched his shrivelled hand. Instinctively he pulled it back and shook his head. Didn't she know he had leprosy? She smiled and took his hand again and gently squeezed. With the other hand she offered him her bottled drink. He drank slowly at first and then, tipping his head back, quickly gulped it all down, savouring the cool liquid. It spilled over, streaking down his dusty face. The bottle now empty, she took money out of her pockets and gave it to him. Then she pulled out some biscuits and gave him those. But what he noticed most of all—as she did those things she smiled. And the smile reminded him of his mother.

She stepped aside and he shuffled by her. Throughout the encounter not a word was spoken. He didn't look back but he knew she was watching him as he shambled into the distance. The money and food would last him for a few more days and maybe then it would be the end. But it wasn't just the food he was grateful for; it was everything about her, her touch, her smile, and her unspoken thoughts. He knew she saw him as a person like herself. He didn't know who she was and he knew they would never meet again. He walked into the distance just a little straighter and just a little prouder.

For the woman, this encounter on a March day in 1990 set in motion a chain of events that would change her life for ever.

Chapter 1   My First Trip to India

Alighting from the air-conditioned plane at Mumbai Airport was like walking into a brick wall. I thought the jet engines were still thrusting at full blast but then realised it was the intense suffocating heat. I soon became so thirsty I could have drunk from a puddle. My clothes stuck to me as, with my companions, I walked towards the cluster of corrugated iron-roofed sheds ahead of us. A strong smell of curry permeated the air.

The airport was without air-conditioning and offered no relief from the heat. All around was the hustle and bustle of a cosmopolitan community that moved about with no seeming sense of purpose. Armed guards, carrying old-fashioned rifles, weaved threateningly amongst the milling crowds. Crows flew overhead, mosquitoes were all over.

My companions and I stood speechless unable to take in the chaos of it all. It was so unlike the ordered world of Heathrow Airport we'd left nine hours earlier. This was my first long haul journey away from my family and I welled up inside thinking of that last sight of them as I waved goodbye. I couldn't stop myself shaking. I wasn't alone in my fears. Coming from the backwaters of East Anglia, we were all apprehensive about what would happen next.

Everywhere were endless queues for customs and passport control. Incomprehensible Indian voices shouted and gesticulated for us to join one of them. Pressed forward by those behind, we reached the front where our passports were snatched from us to be replaced by slips of paper that we clutched tightly afraid we might lose them.

We were all hungry and tired and in need of the washroom. I was volunteered to check out the nearby 'Ladies'; a thin barefooted female attendant in a tattered and faded sari sat at the door. Her face was the texture of creased leather and expressionless. On payment of a small tip she offered me two sheets of toilet paper. She beckoned me to follow as head bent low she scuffed her way across the dirty wet floor. We passed another woman curled up and sleeping against one wall, impervious to the banging of cubicle doors and those stepping over her. The attendant opened the door of a vacant cubicle for me, disturbing a cockroach that scuttled out of sight. I was grateful to see a conventional toilet bowl. I'd been warned that some toilets in India were no more than holes in the floor. The attendant wiped the seat and left me to it. I coped with the necessities; my feet raised up off the floor.

I kept thinking, "I must be mad". Here I was, plain Pat Atkinson: approaching middle age: happily married to Brian: mother of two lively teenage daughters, Jo and Claire: flying half way round the world on behalf of an East Anglian charity. I was employed by the charity to set up community care projects in the Norwich area. So what was I doing in India?

I thought back to a morning six months earlier when I was tutoring a class of students on different aspects of caring for others. There I was, in full flow, when the door flew open and the charity director burst in. "Pat, you're interested in India, aren't you?" he said. "All my life," I replied without questioning why he was asking me. "I thought as much. The charity is looking at a project for India and we need a small team to visit and to investigate. One of the team members has dropped out due to ill health and I'd like you to go instead." I kept silent about my own chequered health history. This opportunity was too good to miss.

"But, if you accept, there's a snag," he added. "You will need to raise £1,000 personally for the start of the project, plus pay your India costs". He explained the visit was scheduled for March 1990. The project brief was to evaluate the feasibility of the construction of a new school for disabled children in Madurai in the state of Tamil Nadu, South India. The finance would come from this charity but the project would be managed through an overseas charity. Getting through the rest of the day was a struggle. I was so excited I couldn't wait to rush home and discuss it with the family.

If I could have foreseen the future, I might have backed off but the desire to visit India blinkered me to all obstacles. Since the age of nine, I'd been convinced God wanted me to serve in India as a Missionary but, having been rejected by a Missionary Society in my twenties, it had become a long forgotten dream and my life since had taken other paths.

On hearing the news, Brian and the girls were all for it. Would they have been so eager had they known where it would lead? Over the next few months, with the assistance of my home church, St Stephen's in Norwich I raised the £1,000. Although each of us in the travelling group had met at the odd briefing meeting beforehand, it was only on the flight that I became fully acquainted with my companions. We were to have our differences in the future, but on this trip we bonded together well as we learned to cope with being in this strange, overcrowded and very hot country.

By the time I returned to the group following my encounter with the cockroaches, my companions were sitting in the airport restaurant. Unwashed crockery littered the grubby tables, spilt food and drink littered the floor. The food on the self-service counter was uncovered and provided a landing ground for numerous flies. Hungry as we all were, we opted for bars of chocolate and bottled water. Our internal flight to Trivandrum, the next staging post en route to Madurai, was still six hours away. There was nowhere comfortable to sit or lie; springs and stuffing spilled out of the few seats provided.

Most of the people in my group were evangelical Christians and one suggested that we have a prayer together. We held hands around the table and placed ourselves in God's care. We all felt comforted after this and readier for what lay ahead.

The internal flight took off at early light and below us through the smog and heat haze we caught a glimpse of the shanty town that stretched between the international and domestic airports of Mumbai. It was a drab carpet, an unending mixture of shades of dark brown and the red rust of corrugated iron, relieved intermittently by a sudden glint as the sun caught a clean sheet of metal. I came to realise that Mumbai epitomised the paradox that is India. From shanty slums to magnificent hotels and office blocks: from ramshackle street stalls to modern department stores: from ragged clothes to the latest fashions: old and new and good and bad co-existing in a chaotic maelstrom.

As soon as we touched down in Trivandrum, close to the southern tip of India and several hundred miles from Mumbai, there was a rush to leave the plane. The passengers ignored the 'Keep seat belts fastened' sign and jostled one another for a prime position in the aisles. Once off the plane there was a stampede to the terminal.

We walked outside into almost forty-degree heat and soon became parched with thirst—a thirst that would remain with me throughout our visit. Maintaining the huge daily liquid intake necessary to prevent dehydration was difficult. Feelings of dryness in nasal cavities and throat, and even in the eyes, became the norm.

We were met by a representative of our host organisation in Trivandrum who took us to waiting taxis. As we were about to get in, we were stopped by a tiny lady under four feet tall. She gestured with the stump of her leprosy-ridden hand to her empty mouth. She was skin and bone. Twenty-two years later I can still see her face.

As we drove out of the airport, the dust and the air burned into my lungs making it difficult to breathe. We drove through the town and then we were in the suburbs. Lining the dusty roads on both sides were shacks—people's homes—some barely more than sacking around a wooden frame, others nothing more than a space on the pavement. Loud music was blaring out all around and the pungent smell of curry seemed to have followed us from Mumbai. It invaded our senses; it soaked into our clothes; it impregnated everything we ate and drank including the Pepsi Cola.

Everywhere people—walking, squatting, lying, and all so incredibly thin. Among them dogs and cattle roamed at will. I was numb with shock. And then, just as I thought it couldn't get any worse, we came upon our first stonebreakers. Along the sides of the road, under roughly made palm shelters and surrounded by lumps of granite, the stonebreakers, mostly women, wielded their hammers, chipping away hour after hour, day after day streaming with sweat in the unremitting heat. By the time we reached our luxury hotel the tears were streaming down my face. Why had I come here? I didn't want to stay. Somehow I had to get home.

So what changed? How did this horror transform into the deep love I have for India. I suppose it began as I got to know the people.

My air-conditioned room at the hotel was ornately furnished and equipped with more comforts than I was used to at home. I pulled back the covers of the large double bed and stroked the cool soft sheets. The view from my window was of palm trees laden with coconuts. In the distance was the calmest, bluest sea I'd ever seen and a golden beach dotted with wooden fishing boats. It was as pretty as any picture in a travel brochure. I wallowed in the luxury of a warm bath and tried to wash away the grime and the memories of the journey. Later, as our group sat on the balcony in the quiet of the evening enjoying a delicious meal, the sights we'd experienced just a few hours ago seemed a distant nightmare. The only sound that jarred in the quiet of the evening was the chip chip chip beneath our balcony. Our host from the local charity apologised for the disturbance: "It's the stonebreakers." He explained that the stones were delivered and had to be broken into chippings before they could be used. It was a task carried out by the Dalits, the so-called untouchables. Most of the workers were women and for twelve hours work a day they received enough pay to feed a small family. They worked every day without exception, as no work meant no food. I looked over the wall in the fading light. The squatting, emaciated shapes brought back the horror of what I had seen on the journey from the airport. I slept fitfully in the soft sheets, wanting to do something to help, but not sure whether I had the strength.

I rose early and before breakfast strolled down to the hotel beach to clear my head and video the scenery. The air was fresher with a light breeze blowing. Dotted on the sea were the wooden boats of the fishermen. Close to, I could see they were no more than hollowed-out logs propelled manually with paddles. A few fishermen had managed to buy outboard motors, the weight of which settled their boats low in the water. I watched as they hauled in their nets set the night before, singing as they did so, and then coasting into the beach on the breakers to unload their catch to sell to waiting customers.

As I videoed, some of them came nearer. They crowded in closer and reached out to touch the camera. I backed away but they pressed forward chattering and laughing, pointing at the camera. Suddenly, I realised there was nothing to be afraid of. They were merely curious. Soon I was showing them the video I'd taken and we started to make each other understood by a mixture of sign language and broken English. I showed them photos of my daughters and some indicated they had children too. Enjoying their company, little by little my fears evaporated. I began to see that despite the differences in our life circumstances, our hopes and dreams were the same. They had families and friends, cared for their children, wanted to be happy, and enjoyed a good laugh. On that beach, surrounded by these excitable fun loving men, I began to fall in love with India. They were so friendly that I accepted their offer of a fish barbecue for our entire group for the modest sum of 50p per head. We held it on the beach that evening—our last dinner before the journey to Madurai.

The distance from Trivandrum to Madurai is about 300 miles and our transport was a rickety minibus driven by two delightful drivers. The bus looked as if it had been rescued from a scrapyard and we had serious doubts about whether it would make the distance. We squeezed in with our luggage and set off, in the now familiar heat of forty degrees centigrade, along National Highway 47. The mini bus shook and rattled making us all feel ill. Almost from the start, we suffered acute thirst that worsened as the journey progressed. We were also feeling sick; probably the effect of the anti-malarial pills we were taking. My senses throughout were battered by the poverty around us. The villages along the route merged into one another, all teeming with scrawny underfed people who laughed and waved as we passed by. The wooden shacks that lined both sides of the highway were of different shapes and sizes but were all the same monotonous sandy brown colour, most of them thatched with banana leaves. Open sewer drains ran alongside the road and, at intervals, little wayside shops interrupted the monotony, selling water and soft drinks, usually Pepsi Cola, to passing travellers. Our pleas to stop for drinks to quench our thirst met with cries from our drivers, 'We stop soon. We stop soon', but we travelled nearly 200 miles before we pulled in.

I don't know the name of the village and I would never be able to find it again. It was no different from the others we'd passed through. It was the same higgledy-piggledy squalor of shacks but it was here that my love affair with the people of India, which began with the fishermen on the hotel beach, was consummated. It was here that my life was irrevocably changed. We untangled ourselves and got out of the mini bus laughing and joking eager to stretch our legs. One of the drivers hurried into the local store for drinks that we snatched from his hands when he returned. Drink in hand, I moved slightly apart from the others to seek some shade.

It was then I noticed a young man leaning very heavily on a stick. His legs seemed too weak to support his body as he walked in a crab-like motion. The look of hopelessness in his eyes was devastating. He hardly glanced at us as he passed. There was blood around his mouth, open sores all over his body. His rasping cough told me he was in the terminal stages of tuberculosis. Through the ragged cloth around his shoulders I could see the skeleton of his rib cage. I think he was about fourteen or fifteen, but he was no bigger than a seven-year-old. He was not the first beggar I'd encountered. From the moment we stepped off the plane we had found ourselves the target of outstretched hands and clutching fingers. We usually turned away, but it was different with this young man. I had to follow him. He was like a walking corpse. There was something about his expressionless eyes deeply sunk in their sockets – an emptiness, a hopelessness - that reached into me and tore at my heart.

I drew closer to him and handed him my bottle of drink. As I did so, I went to touch his hand, a hand that was no more than a diseased stump. He pulled it away and shook his head, probably thinking he would infect me with leprosy. I knew that wasn't possible, so I took his hand in mine and steadied him while he started to drink slowly at first, then tipping his head back and gulping it down. When he finished, I emptied my pockets and handed him some biscuits and a little money. As he took them, his eyes filled with tears and then he was gone, dragging himself along. To this day I can see his face and feel his arm—an arm which seemed to have no flesh on it. He broke my heart. My fear of India left me. I knew where I wanted to be—where I had to be. I wanted to help these hurting people. No, it was more than help them—I wanted to love them.

A willingness to help was one thing, but exactly how was another. What did I know of this people's history, its problems, its religion or its culture? Why did such vast numbers live in abject poverty when around them others lived in splendid opulence? I had a lot to learn, and after twenty two years, I am still learning.

Society in India is structured on a caste system where everyone holds a specific place in a rigid hierarchy. The system is complex, intricately interwoven with the Hindu religion and the concepts of purity and pollution, reincarnation and karma. The Hindus in India were originally divided into a number of exclusive hereditary groups, usually by their occupations, and given the names of castes by the Portuguese settlers. There are approximately seventy castes, determined by varying degrees of purity and pollution, the 'purest' caste being the Brahmins. To marry or work outside one's caste is forbidden, not by law, but by social convention. Taking food or socialising with a lower caste invites contamination. Purity is of great concern to Indians and death can contaminate an entire family. There are many cleansing rituals. One of them, banned during British rule, and fortunately now rare—*sati*—required a widow to follow her deceased husband onto the funeral pyre.

It is believed that thousands of successive births through reincarnation are necessary to ascend from a lower to a higher caste. It is *karma*, one's destiny, determined by an accumulation of good and bad acts. A good life will expiate one's sins and the reward will be a better life next time around.

The Dalits are the exception. They are considered so polluted that not only can they never be pure but they will be a source of pollution to anyone with whom they come into contact. They are 'outcasts', excluded from the caste system. They will always be Dalits regardless of what they achieve in life and how many times they are reincarnated. You may wonder why they put up with a system which dictates that they will be eternally oppressed. They do it because this is the only world they know and they cannot conceive of another. The fact that they are such a docile and accepting people is a significant barrier to social change.

In a belief system which says you can be defiled by certain jobs, the Dalits do the work that would make those of other castes unclean. They handle sewage disposal, clean the waste from latrines, and sift through the raw sewage looking for anything they might sell. They are hotel workers, rag-pickers and street cleaners. Interestingly, they play drums in the temple processions as they are the only ones who will touch animal skins. For many, the death of a Dalit is no more significant than the death of a rat. The Dalit's lot is to live in unsanitary, overcrowded and diseased slum conditions. There are degrees of status within the Dalit community; at the very bottom are those women who do not even have the right to wear a blouse under their sari.

I knew nothing of this at the time and, as we travelled on to Madurai, I said very little to my companions. The only picture in my head was the boy we left behind at the comfort stop. The sight of him hobbling into the distance haunted me.

I needed to know more but where to start? A desire was kindled within me to do something—but what? I felt powerless and inadequate. All I knew, was God had spoken to me through that boy. He had walked away from me, but I knew with absolute certainty there was no way I could walk away from him.

Chapter 2   Early Dreams of India

I was born several weeks prematurely, in Tunbridge Wells, two years after the end of World War II. None of the doctors thought I would survive and my mother was rushed overnight to a specialist care unit in a London hospital. My recollections before the age of eight are vague. All I remember is that my early childhood was a carefree one and I adored my parents. My father was a Warrant Officer in the Royal Air Force which meant we moved frequently from posting to posting. My education was constantly disrupted and I attended a new school every year or so; friendships were short-lived and I never put down any roots. It all seemed normal and didn't bother me. At that young age friends could be quickly made and quickly forgotten. As far as I knew this was the way everyone lived.

When I was about eight years old, the family returned to the UK from Germany, to live in Bath. It was here I entered the happiest period of my childhood. By then I had two brothers Keith and Paul. My youngest brother, Ian, wasn't born until I was sixteen. I was drawn to the countryside. I loved its solitude and my only desire was to spend as much time as possible building hides, climbing trees and wandering through the woods and fields. I'd ramble for miles along country lanes and footpaths and through Bath's beautiful Victoria Park, lost in a wonderland of my own making. The silence, disturbed only by the sound of the birds and the rustle of the wind in the trees, seemed to encompass a world that went on forever. Walking in the country is a pleasure that has never left me; it is during these walks that I find peace and a renewed energy and sense of direction.

I enrolled in the local primary school and it was there I formed a crush on the local curate. He was a tall, dark, attractive man twenty years my senior. I followed him everywhere hoping he would notice me and ask me to do something for him. This led me to the church of St. John the Baptist at Bathwick, where he took the services. The church was High Anglican and came complete with all the bells and smells. My parents were not regular churchgoers and had not prepared me for this. However, I found that the High Church ritual appealed to my embryonic sense of spirituality and an awareness of people and their needs. I felt I was in the right place. I still look on that church as my spiritual home. I began to attend the early morning service and help the lady who made the breakfasts. She was a friendly grey-haired lady in her early eighties with a heart-warming smile. After breakfast I sat with her during the service. When asked about her role in the church her reply was always, "I only make the tea." Her humble dedication to others made a great impact on me.

I wrote poems as a child. In terms of structure and emotional feel they weren't classic poetry, but when I read them now I'm surprised at their maturity. The following poem I wrote shortly before my confirmation: it captures exactly my feelings on the spiritual path I was travelling:

> Jesus, why do you bother with me?
> What possible use to you can I be?
> Every parable you ever told,
> Seems to condemn me sevenfold.
> Why do you bother with me?

> Jesus, all right, I'll give it a try;
> You seem to want me, I'll never know why.
> I've committed almost every sin you can name
> And probably I'll do it again;
> Are you sure you really want me?

> Jesus, couldn't I just hold your hand?
> There's a lot to face that I don't understand.
> You're smiling I see;
> Yes, Lord it must be
> That you truly, really want me.

My childlike faith took a giant stride towards maturity on the day a lady missionary came to the church to talk about India. What a revelation to me. Being a Christian was easy if it just meant attending church on a Sunday but true faith had to be much more than that. She talked of reaching out to the poor, the lame and the lepers, and as I listened, a blanket of warmth engulfed me. By the time her talk was over, I knew with absolute certainty, that God wanted me to be a missionary in India. It's easy to shrug this off as silly adolescent emotion born of the moment but the desire stayed with me.

As my faith grew I was determined to be confirmed when I was eleven. I had been baptized as a baby but confirmation was special; this was my own commitment to God. My parents were happy enough for me to attend church but although I pestered them, they had no wish to become involved themselves. These were happy days, but it was at my confirmation that I experienced the first symptoms of the illness that was to have such a debilitating effect on my teenage years and my dreams for the future. I was kneeling at the altar rail, a copy of the catechism stuffed inside my dress, terrified I might forget the words to the responses, when suddenly a pain like a piercing knife seared through my knees and hip. I wanted to stand up it hurt so much but, flushed as I was with my innocent faith, I was determined not to let God down and remained kneeling. The same agonising pain reappeared intermittently over the next year or so but visits to the doctor only resulted in being brushed aside with the diagnosis, 'adolescent growing pains.'

I passed the eleven plus and attended an all-girls grammar school, the Bath Diocesan Girls School, where I was extremely happy and met my lifelong friend Mary. However, my increasing involvement in sport exacerbated the pains in my joints. The realisation of my parents that the pains were quite serious finally dawned at a netball match. I was goal shooter - partly because I was taller than everyone else - earning me the nickname 'Lanks'. One time, the ball came to me at a difficult angle for a clear shot. It was at a critical moment in the game, and someone called, 'Go for it Lanks!' As I twisted awkwardly for a better throw, I felt a stab of pain in my legs and hip. I doubled up in pain. It was impossible to jump and I collapsed to the ground in agony.

My parents made an urgent appointment with the doctor but, as before, he couldn't find anything physically wrong and started probing my mental state. Was I unhappy at school – or maybe at home? Did I have boyfriend trouble? The whole visit was inconclusive terminating with the same diagnosis that it was just growing pains. My mother took me back several times in the next year because by now the pain was so bad she would often find me curled up on my bed sobbing.

This went on for about a year until I woke one morning and couldn't move from the waist down. I was shaking. I thought I was paralyzed. The pain in my legs was unrelenting and I lay in my bed, tears streaming down my face, with my mother holding me and trying to calm me down. It took both my parents to lift me and take me to the doctor's surgery. The doctor was still not convinced that the pain was physical. "I know there's something going on in her life that she's hiding," he said and told my parents it was a form of hysteria. My father, dissatisfied with the GP's diagnosis, spoke to one of the doctors at his RAF base, who came to see me that same day. Half an hour later I was in an ambulance. It took a few days of tests to diagnose acute Still's Disease, a form of rheumatoid arthritis. The prognosis was that I would be in hospital for some considerable time.

I was immediately encased in a plaster bed, dosed with painkillers and forced to use a bedpan. I lay on my stomach on a wedge for several hours a day so I couldn't see what was going on around me. I couldn't feed myself and had to rely on the nurses. My only visitors were my parents. The saddest thing was that no-one from the church came to see me. My only friend was Flossie in the next bed. We both gazed out on a ward of patients that to our young eyes appeared ancient. Some were comatose with tubes poking out from under the sheets pumping strange liquids into bags. When someone screamed out in the night the nurses would hurriedly pull screens around their bed. Patients would come and go, but I felt as though I was in a prison from which there was no escape. My life was hopeless. Then one night Flossie disappeared. No-one would tell me where she'd gone and I felt as though a shadow had fallen across my life. Now, with no-one of my age to talk to, I felt so alone.

Picking up on whispered conversations between my parents and the doctors, and on the evasive answers to my questions, I was haunted by the nightmare that I might never walk again. Later, when things began to improve my mother, sitting by my hospital bed holding my hand, said, "You know love, on the first day we were given the news of how serious your illness was, your Dad went home and locked himself in the bathroom and I heard him sobbing his heart out." In those bleak moments of loneliness and despair I dwelt a lot on God. My illness had a profound impact on my attitude. It brought an awareness that finding contentment in the simple pleasures of life was more important than money and fame.

I missed so much of the life most teenagers of my day took for granted. Not for me those early teenage parties, sleepovers, new dance crazes such as the Twist, miniskirts, and most of all developing relationships with boys. I also had to forego the trips to the theatre that I enjoyed so much. Our home was near the Theatre Royal in Bath and, through a friend, I'd wheedled my way into the good books of the theatre manager who, in exchange for my walking his dog, would give me a free ticket for a seat in the gods for the latest production. Pantomime was a great favourite of mine (and still is) and my idol was Norman Stanley, a comedian, who appeared at the Theatre Royal every year. I would cheer from my seat when he made an entrance and wait at the stage door after the show for his autograph. "Not again," he'd say. "Oh all right then," and he would sign the creased programme I thrust under his nose. He wrote to me a few times whilst I was in hospital and this was a great comfort and encouragement to me.

When I finally emerged from the plaster bed I was taken each day to the hot springs in Bath and lowered into the waters. Gradually movement in my legs returned until, after three months, I was able to walk unsteadily around the ward. I helped the ward sister with the menial chores and on occasions accompanied the doctor on his rounds. I think it was helping those who were suffering more than me that pointed my thoughts to becoming a nurse. Somehow, fixed in my mind was the idea that this would be useful to me as a missionary in India. Although I was discharged after four and a half months, the disease flared up repeatedly and I was nearly fourteen before I returned to school regularly, having missed a year of studies.

I'd hardly readjusted to school life in Bath when Dad announced he'd been posted to RAF Halton in Buckinghamshire. Another move and another school. It broke my heart to leave Bath, my school, and my church and end the friendships that were just beginning. Fourteen is a sensitive age to undergo an upheaval of this kind and I felt my life had been devastated. (Years later I return to Bath several times a year, still in touch with my school friend Mary and, more recently, with other ex-classmates at Reunion evenings.)

I moved from a girls' grammar school of 350 pupils to a mixed comprehensive in Wendover with 1500. From the minute I arrived I was the subject of ridicule. I limped badly and sometimes had to use my crutches. I often had to sit down because of the pain. It was hard to break into the established circles of friends. Parties or nights out were still out of the question and I was still burdened with regular physiotherapy. One teacher said, "Not another Air Force child! What's the point of teaching you for just a few months?" and she made me sit at the back of the class. I felt an outcast at school, always on my own in the playground, teased and bullied because of my limping. Looking back, I see how all this helped me to empathise later in life with the untouchable children in India.

Instead of doing O and A Levels as I would have done in Bath, I was placed in a remedial class. When my parents complained, it was suggested that I take a vocational course to help me cope with my disabilities in the longer term. I left school twelve days before my fifteenth birthday with no qualifications and went to train as a GPO telephonist. They were pleased to accept me as my disabilities helped them to fulfil their legal requirement to employ a percentage of disabled people. After six months of probation in the Aylesbury Exchange my health improved and I was able to move to the private sector as a telephonist-cum-receptionist.

Because I made so many visits to outpatients for physiotherapy, the hospital chapel in Buckinghamshire became my church. There, to help the chaplain, I learnt to play the organ after a fashion. Although my experience with church had not always been positive, my faith was still strong and I was more determined than ever to be a missionary.

Before long, another RAF posting took us to Carlisle and the move helped shed the bad memories of the past years. Carlisle was good. My mother started an amateur dramatics group, an interest she'd kept up since joining a variety troupe during her service in the Air Force before her marriage. She staged revues and pantomimes and as a family we got to know the Music Hall artist Wee Georgie Wood. I even performed with him as a member of his singing group the 'Woodpeckers'.

By now my health had improved considerably and the clergy of my new church encouraged my desire to be a missionary and reinforced my ambition to train as a nurse. Because of my father's connections it was natural to apply to the Royal Air Force. However, my medical history returned to haunt me. Even though I could pass the entrance exams I failed the medical for the RAF and went on to fail three more medicals for entry to civilian hospitals. Finally, in desperation, I applied to the Army who accepted me at the Colchester Military Hospital on a State Enrolled Nursing Course.

From day one, I struggled. I hated the marching, which seemed to have no relevance to nursing. More than anything, I hated the lack of moral standards shown by some of my colleagues. This was the late sixties and drugs and promiscuity were commonplace. I didn't sleep around; I didn't take drugs; and, to cap it all, I went to church. The culture was alien to me and, once again, I found myself an outsider. I spent a lot of time on my own in the barracks. Being not quite eighteen I could not start my general training so I spent the first few months on endless drill. It was drill, drill and more drill, but that led to me being on parade for Winston Churchill's funeral, a very proud moment in my life.

Despite my unhappiness, I stuck with the training and, after two years, I qualified as an army nurse. I was about to take the exam to qualify as a state registered nurse when disaster struck again. I was nursing a child with rheumatic fever. Three days later I had a sore throat and all my joints were swollen. I woke in the early hours drenched with sweat and with agonizing pains not only in my hips and knees but in my arms. The Stills disease had returned. I was admitted immediately to hospital for what was to be four months of treatment followed by a medical discharge from the Army and an end, it seemed, to all I'd worked for. I was twenty years old with a calliper on my leg, without a State Nursing qualification, without a job and desperately lonely. My parents were in Carlisle and I was in Colchester.

I applied to St Christopher's Hospice in London where I'd previously done some placement work and they took me on as a volunteer for nine months to help develop bereavement training. During this time I obtained a Diploma in Counselling from the Westminster Pastoral Foundation. At the end of that period I was broke. I had no choice but to return home to my parents. Optimistically, I followed up an earlier application for overseas work with the Church Missionary Society. Their rejection was final: my medical record and my lack of a state nursing qualification ruled me out.

I sobbed when I read the letter. I lay in bed that night feeling bitter and cheated. My childhood dream of working in India had been shattered.

Chapter 3   From Bingo Caller to Deaconess

I found a clerical job but still felt depressed. I tried to lift my spirits by joining in once more with my mother's theatricals—singing and playing the trumpet. One night, at one of the shows, there was a man in the audience by the name of Frederick Thrower who ran a holiday camp. He liked my performance and after the show he came back stage to speak to me. "I've heard that you've had a bit of a rough ride, but you've obviously got a lot of talent and I'm looking for someone who can take care of the medical needs of the holidaymakers," he said. "But I'm not State qualified," I replied. "I know, but you have sufficient qualifications to look after the medical requirements I have in mind. In addition, you play a mean trumpet. You could join with the dance band in the evening and run the children's entertainments programme in the day. Are you interested?"

On hearing the holiday camp was at Gorleston, I thought why not? After all, I'd always wanted to go to Scotland! If my hearing had been better and I'd paid more attention to geography at school, I might not have jumped at the chance so eagerly. A few days later, I found myself travelling not to *Gordonstoun* in the Scottish highlands but to *Gorleston* Super Holiday Camp in the much more prosaic East Anglia. It was a small upmarket camp (later renamed Elmhurst Court), restricted to 400 adults and twenty-two children. I was part of an entertainments team of three and spent my days organising games and outings and frequently being pushed fully clothed into the pool. I worked non-stop. When I finished with the children in the day, I played the trumpet or harmonica and sang with Bernard, Rolly and George in the evening. We were *The Bernard Heard Trio and Pat*. If that wasn't enough, I was dance MC, dance partner, bingo caller, and general dogsbody. I worked fourteen hours or more a day, seven days a week. By the end of the season I was exhausted, but much stronger. I met people from all walks of life. I played trumpet for Sid James in a sketch he performed. I rubbed shoulders with comedians Mike and Bernie Winters and singer Engelbert Humperdink. During those years I discovered I could get along with anyone. It was great grounding for the church ministry and, as I always say, bingo calling is the best training I know for a preacher. Being discharged from the army and rejected as a missionary had badly bruised my self-esteem, but the work at the holiday camp restored my self-confidence. They were some of the happiest days of my life.

Unfortunately the holiday camp only provided summer work, so I decided to go home for the winter. But I was so homesick for Norfolk that I returned after three days to look for work around Great Yarmouth. My jobs ranged from working at the Birds Eye factory as a Pea Inspector (that lasted one day), to night care nursing and serving in a department store. I drifted back to attending church in a lukewarm way and was encouraged by the vicar to study for O and A levels.

In 1970, at the end of my third season at the holiday camp, I went to work for the Gas Board under a temporary contract as part of the nationwide North Sea Gas Conversions. My supervisor was a man called Brian Atkinson. My first impression was not favourable. He wore dark trousers, a white shirt, and a beige cardigan. He had a pen behind his ear and a look that suggested he'd missed his breakfast. I didn't think I was going to like him at all. But gradually, as I came to know him better, I fell in love. I found beneath the shy exterior a kind, loving and gentle man. He was steady and reliable and, given the insecurity of my life until then, he was what I needed. Over the years, I know without his support and rock solid steadiness I would never have achieved all that I have.

We were married in 1971 and I did not return to the holiday camp. Brian and I moved to London for a year on secondment for the Gas Board. It was a rough first year as we travelled to and from Norfolk to Brian's parents at weekends. Part of the attraction of those visits was watching the Norwich City Football Club home games. Brian was an avid supporter and his enthusiasm rubbed off on me.

After marrying Brian I stopped going to church. It was not a deliberate decision but Brian was not a churchgoer and our itinerant lifestyle did not provide a settled existence in one place. I was happy and contented with married life and church did not seem relevant to either of us. God was no longer an important part of my life and things were going very well without Him. Yet there were times of reflection when, despite my happy life, I felt there was something missing.

When the work in London finished we returned to Norfolk to settle in Norwich. I found myself drawn to attending the occasional service at the Cathedral. It was on one of my visits that I passed an elderly down-and-out asleep on a bench in the cloisters. He was there a week later and again a week after that and I became so concerned that I stayed behind after a service to speak to one of the clergy (who is no longer there). "I'm really worried about the old man outside on the bench," I said. Before I could say more, he replied, "You're right, I'm worried about him too.....he so lowers the tone of the Close." I was stunned at the response. The old man needed love and care; those two words 'love' and 'care' echoed in my head for days.

Shortly after, browsing in the Careers Section of Norwich library, I spotted on the third shelf, sticking out from the other books, one with a blue cover. I picked it out. It was about the Deaconess Order in the Anglican Church, an order of women who committed themselves to work for the poor, the sick, the old and the lonely. Many of them worked in hospitals as chaplains. A picture of the old man came to mind and the words 'love and care' re-echoed. I started attending church again. In 1976 my daughter Jo was born and in that same year I began to plan for admission to the Deaconess Order. I knew I couldn't apply without some qualifications so I returned to my lapsed studies. In the first year I sat three O levels in Religious Studies, English Language and Sociology and, a year later, an A level in Human Biology. In 1978, my second daughter Claire was born. The same year I was accepted by the Anglican Examining Body for a three year external Ministerial Training Course to become a Deaconess.

As a trainee Deaconess, along with my theological studies, I started and continued for the next seven years to work as an unpaid chaplain at an NHS hospital. During that time, I also worked nights in a nursing home to earn some money for the family. The chaplaincy work was only supposed to be for three hours a week but sickness among the other chaplains meant I was working long hours alone without a superior and had to learn from my own mistakes. Offering comfort to the patients in the hospital satisfied some of my nursing instincts but there was one aspect of the work that increasingly disturbed and upset me.

One of my duties was handling requests to baptise babies, newly born, usually premature, and so sickly they were unlikely to survive for more than a few hours. Because the babies had breathed, they were given an identity and a birth and death certificate. This was of comfort to the parents at a traumatic time and meant they could give the baby a funeral and a burial—a great help in the grieving process. One night I received an urgent call to baptise a baby born at twenty-six weeks, who had survived for less than an hour. I arranged a full funeral and the parents were consoled in their grief by the chaplaincy staff, who treated them with kindness and consideration. Three weeks later, a twenty-seven week premature baby was born but, in this instance, the baby never breathed. The law at that time was specific—it would change three years later—babies born without signs of life before twenty-eight weeks were pre-stillbirth and no different to a miscarried foetus.

These dear little limp beings had formed features, arms and legs, but, because they had not taken a breath, they did not legally exist. The parents never questioned what would happen to their baby as a nurse took it from the mother's arms. All I could do was watch, helpless to soften the grief of the parents, knowing that for this baby there would be no baptism, no birth certificate, no death certificate and no funeral. I thought of my own premature birth; I thought of Jo and Claire and I wept for the parents. The parents were left to deal with their unresolved grief without the closure that would have come with a funeral. But why was this small human being considered nothing, simply because it didn't breathe at birth? And why were the needs of these parents different from the needs of the parents whose baby had happened to breathe for a few minutes. I did some research and found this practice was commonplace throughout the country. The hospital did arrange for 'sensitive disposal' by burial or cremation but the parents were not involved.

Once I realised how prevalent it was I contacted the Stillbirth and Neonatal Death Society (SANDS) who said, "You're fighting the battle we're fighting.

We don't know what to do about it either." I raised it with some of the medical staff. One Consultant said to me, "If a baby doesn't breathe then it's dead. It's just a foetus. It doesn't matter to the parents what happens to it. I don't see women weeping and wailing." But I did. And I resolved to do something about it. I approached the vicar of my own church and, after many discussions, I was able to negotiate the allocation of a small area between the graves in the churchyard where I could bury the babies myself. I found a hospital porter and a couple of midwives who were in sympathy with me. With their help and a carpenter who volunteered to make little coffins, we were able to bury the babies and as I buried each one I prayed for them and their families. The parents were not aware of the details but I was able to reassure them their baby's body had been tenderly cared for.

It was unconventional and not done without some opposition, but I was supported by the Stillbirth Society and through them, in 1989, Anglia Television picked up the story and made a documentary (*Journeys*) about what was happening. To quote the documentary, "What she was doing was unusual and unprecedented, but gradually other hospitals began to follow Pat's example, and eventually the need for documentation and legislation for the burial of stillborn infants was recognised." My local Bishop raised the issue in the House of Lords and eventually legislation was passed which allowed the necessary documentation for burial of stillborn babies in church or municipal cemeteries. The Bishop had cleverly made the point that as the babies had no registration documents to prove they had been born, let alone died, in law they did not exist. Therefore, any opposition was about burying 'nothing'. Once the documentation was available, my hospital became the first in the country to buy a plot in a cemetery for these babies and other hospitals followed suit. SANDS invited me to join some others in writing a book called *After Stillbirth: what Happens Next,* which was a standard textbook for nurses for many years.

My busy life at the hospital and the care home plus bringing up a family and completing my Ministerial studies exhausted me and, as there was still no sign of my Chaplaincy post being funded, I had no option but to give up both the chaplaincy and the care home job. I found a job with a charity, which involved organising and running bereavement training. This was similar to the work I'd done in St Christopher's Hospice when I left the Army all those years before. The courses were so successful that a year later I joined the paid staff and I was able to extend my studies to take an Adult Education Teaching Diploma. I was assigned to teaching care staff. I'd been doing this for about a year when, one morning in 1989, the director entered my class with the request that would change my life.

Chapter 4   The Work Begins: Meeting the Children

After this diversion into the details of my early life, it is time to pick up again the narrative of my first trip to India. India is a vast continent and, although it may seem to be a homogenous whole, its states were once separate kingdoms and its peoples and cities distinctly different. On that first visit in 1990, there was little time for me to sightsee and appreciate the magic and contradictions that are India. My experience and work with the children in those early years, was, for the most part, centred in Trivandrum and Madurai; two strongly contrasting cities each with its own individual characteristics and its own language.

Madurai is a city that never sleeps. Situated in the state of Tamil Nadu, it is one of the oldest cities of India, with a population of approximately 3 million (2011 census). The capital of Tamil Nadu is Chennai (Madras). The state has boundless barren plains with water in short supply and in some areas almost non-existent. It is separated from the state of Kerala (whose capital is Trivandrum) by the Western Ghats, a range of mountains running almost the full length of the west coast. The city sprawls on either side of the River Vaigai and is sometimes called the 'Athens of the East'. It is a patchwork of luxurious hotels, tall office blocks, palm-thatched shacks and open sewers. A section of the city I would later come to know well was the large slum where people lived in whatever space they could find.

The city is famous for its temples. It radiates outwards from the Meenakshi Sundareswarar Temple designed to resemble the structure of the heavens. The area around the Temple is the most congested part of the city, buzzing with people, yellow auto rickshaws, bicycles, handcarts, oxen and the occasional elephant. It is a hodgepodge of stalls and shops selling everything from bananas to saris with no more than a foot of space between them. Traders hawk their wares, tailors sit at their ironing boards, street children tug at coat-tails and thousands of people sleep rough on the streets. Many of them have never been to school; over half of them can neither read nor write.

Above all is the noise: a cacophony of traffic, horns, bells, train sirens and temple music that continues uninterrupted until the early hours of the morning. You cannot move in any direction without stepping aside to avoid a person, a bicycle, a rickshaw, or a cow. It is one hot steamy mass of humanity. The people are conservative in their values and traditional dress is still preferred to Western clothing. They are friendly and easy going, although if they wish to insult you, their language has a rich vocabulary for the purpose.

Madurai frequently suffers from power cuts. On one terrifying occasion, I was stuck in a hotel lift with no one but the liftboy for company. Unfortunately, the only air supply to the lift was through a non-functioning electric pump and both of us were banging on the doors screaming for help. By the time rescue came I was struggling to breathe. Since then I have walked up and down thousands and thousands of Indian stairs, avoiding lifts whenever possible.

By contrast Trivandrum, although just as crowded, is a more ordered city. Its Indian name is Thiruvananthapuram, which means 'abode of the snake god Anantha'. It has a population approaching 3.5 million (2011 census). It has an international airport and, as it is close to the sea, the local people benefit from the abundance of fish in the backwaters. Kovalam Beach is a noted tourist spot. The city also boasts the Kanakakunnu Palace, a zoo, sports stadia and art galleries; altogether a more sophisticated city than Madurai, more advanced industrially and with better roads and sewage systems. It is a major academic centre and the home of Kerala University. The literacy rate in Trivandrum is said to be over ninety percent.

Kerala is proud of being ahead of the rest of India in welfare provision but this is of course relative; Trivandrum like Madurai has slums and poverty on a scale we would find horrifying. Of the two cities Trivandrum is the cleaner and has considerably fewer beggars on the streets. Whilst the poverty in Tamil Nadu is concentrated in the cities and made evident by the slums, in Kerala it is more of a problem in the rural areas. The predominant religion is Hindu, but Kerala State also has a strong Christian presence. It is said that St Thomas first brought Christianity to Kerala and founded the Martoma Church which is now a major part of Kerala life. There are many other Christian churches in

Trivandrum, in part reflecting the legacy of the Portuguese settlers who came during the 16th century.

There is a strong cultural difference between Madurai and Trivandrum that is hard to define but it results in an underlying animosity. In the early years my regular driver in India was a native of Trivandrum. I could not understand why he took his own food to eat on our visits to Madurai until out of curiosity I asked him. "Madurai dirty…people dirty…food dirty," was his reply. The people of Tamil Nadu have darker complexions and often seem to be considered inferior by the people of Kerala. I was to discover that the majority of bonded and oppressed Hotel Workers in Trivandrum, of which more later, were children from Tamil Nadu State. These cultural differences influenced the attitudes of the children to one another. The children in the Trivandrum projects came from poor rural areas, whereas those in Madurai were from the city streets and slums. Consequently, attempts to mix the two sets of children generally failed—a little like mixing streetwise children from a 21st century city like London with those from an early 20th century welsh-speaking village

The distinct differences between the two cities often meant the need for a different approach in dealing with problems that arose. I was ignorant of all of this on that first visit. Our contacts were filtered through a local charity on which we relied for transport and accommodation arrangements. The charity ran boys' homes and training centres in both towns, including a school for disabled children in Madurai. In Trivandrum it had introduced a rural development project that provided training in basic electrical and carpentry skills. This, together with the issue of basic tool kits, enabled the trainees to establish themselves in their local communities and to make a reasonable living for their families.

Poverty is relative and compared to the slums, from which they came, the boys lived in luxury. The conditions in the homes were spartan but the boys enjoyed the facilities of a dining room and a classroom. They slept in dormitories on wooden beds that were so close together that it was barely possible to squeeze between them. The beds were covered with a simple cloth cover. There were no mattresses because, in India, they are often a breeding place for bugs and generally only found in the tourist hotels.

The children followed a strictly regimented routine which began at 5 am with prayers and washing, followed by study, breakfast, school, dinner, more study, prayers and then bed. The only time for play, if they were lucky, was half an hour before bedtime. The staff did well in creating a safe and secure environment and in providing the education and skills needed by the boys to find employment and sufficient earnings to provide for their families—in short, the sort of life they could not have dreamed of if they had been left to cope in the slums. While the staff members succeeded in helping the boys to achieve these goals, I feared that most of them showed little warmth or affection.

The boys' need for greater love and affection became very apparent in my personal encounters with them. It took me a little time to break down the barriers. Touching was not normal, but once that inhibition was overcome, the boys' reaction was overwhelming. It was probably the first time that an adult had taken time to sit down with them to have fun and they thrived on it. I loved it too, conversing with them in broken English and hand gestures, and giving them individual attention. I was astonished at the simple things they lacked; they only had one comb between them and little access to simple items such as pencils and paper.

The housemother in the Madurai Home was a wonderful lady. In contrast to some of the other staff members, she added a loving touch that made such a difference to the life of the boys. She'd made a small garden outside and encouraged the boys to grow flowers and shrubs in their own little plot. To us in our temperate climate this may seem trivial but in the near drought conditions of Madurai it means watering by bucket several times a day to keep the plants alive.

It soon became apparent to our group from England that there were serious problems affecting the boys' homes in both Trivandrum and Madurai. The Trivandrum Boys' Home was under pressure because its current sponsors were running down their support and, without a new source of funding, the twenty-six resident boys were likely to be homeless within a year. The Madurai

Home was more secure in its funding but the building, and particularly the pantile roof, was in need of significant repair.

Hearing this after my encounters with the boys, emotions began to churn inside me. That evening, at supper with the group, they boiled over. I pleaded with them: "We have to do something…no matter how little. I can't return to the UK and forget all this. No way can we let those boys be returned to the slums." This was all new to me and I felt so inadequate. My skills as a nurse and counsellor were not what were needed to resolve this type of problem.

One of my colleagues on that first trip shared my concerns. Scribbling on a scrap of paper, we calculated that £8 per month would provide food, accommodation, clothing and education for each boy. The figures seemed so minimal I couldn't believe them and I had to keep rechecking my calculations. Was £8 all that was needed to give a child from the slums a better life? It was no more than the price of paperback or CD. It all seemed so simple, sitting in the hotel drinking *Limca*, (a lemon and lime drink). Never mind the detail, I was so fired up nothing could stop me. I also believed it would be possible to raise funds to contribute to the building of the new school and other projects. I decided that when I returned to the UK I would start giving talks to raise money and set up a scheme whereby each boy would have a specific sponsor to provide for his basic needs and education. The governing body of the charity in Trivandrum was enthused at the prospect. As a symbol of our commitment, some of us went out and purchased pencils, pens and colouring books for the children. Small gift—but for children who knew nothing of sophisticated toys, they provided the same thrill and excitement as an X-box or a Wii. I left India determined to make it work. On returning to the UK we set up a small charity to find sponsors for the children and so meet the financial needs of the Indian charity.

Although I was touched emotionally by all the boys, there was one in particular who affected me profoundly. Jacob-Thomas was fourteen years old but looked about eight or nine. He was a beautiful child with a friendly smile that lit up his small face. Yet behind the smile, the huge brown eyes and the exuberance of youth was a haunting sadness. His mother, too ill to work, suffered from fits after being struck on the head by a falling coconut. In addition, he had a seriously disabled sister with learning difficulties. He had no choice but to leave school early and earn whatever he could to look after them. Through the generous provision of donors in the UK, I was able to provide a year's sponsorship of 300 rupees a month to help support his mother and sister so that he could return to school.

By the time of my second visit in September 1991, a colleague and I had enough sponsors for all the boys in the Trivandrum Home and ten boys in the Madurai Home. I was also actively involved with others in raising half the money needed for the school for disabled children.

I explained earlier how the children responded so eagerly and affectionately to my expressions of love and interest. This meant that each successive visit put me on an emotional seesaw as the boys became more accustomed to me and I kept having to leave them. As the barriers disappeared, I spent more and more of my time surrounded by a horde of exuberant boys. Children, once they are loved and allowed to be children, are the same everywhere.

In Madurai the threat of closure receded as funds were found from other sources. Our new charity in England helped by raising money to fund twenty-five boys out of a total of sixty-five. The local Madurai charity completed plans to demolish and rebuild the existing premises providing much improved accommodation. The Home evolved into a cottage-like development of two-roomed thatched huts, each with its own small garden. Each hut accommodated fifteen boys supervised by one set of house parents. Central to the complex was a community hall funded by a one-off gift from another charity.

As the months progressed, my thoughts naturally turned to what would happen to 'my boys', for that is how I thought of them, when they left the Homes. It seemed pointless for them to return to the streets at the age of fifteen without any of the skills needed to earn a living. It was a natural progression for me and the little group in the UK supporting me that we should look at how we could fund an expansion of the training centres already being piloted. Gradually, we were able to increase our funding to finance larger scale training in electrical, plumbing and carpentry skills and the provision of tool kits. Later, when girls were included, we trained them in tailoring and gave them sewing machines.

During those early years it was a delight to see the change in the boys as they matured to adults. They seemed well cared for, although, as my experience grew, I became concerned that all was not as I would like it to be. Not all the children in the homes were orphans and I was strongly of the view that we should establish close contact with their families. Although I have never wavered in this view, it presents its own problems. A typical example occurred early on when two boys were withdrawn from one of the homes by their mothers. Both boys came from desperately poor backgrounds and their mothers had been unable to feed or care for them from an early age. As a rule, single parents find it impossible to raise young children, because if they cannot work the family starves. Where there are two parents and one is chronically sick and unable to work, the position is much the same. When a young boy goes into the home, there is one less mouth to feed. The parent breadwinner can survive more easily, even if only by begging. But the situation changes once the boy turns fourteen. He is then legally able to go out to work and can become a useful source of income for his family.

By the time I became involved with the boys in question they had both left the Home and had found employment, one as a table boy in a hotel and the other as a messenger. The boys were not being exploited. It was just that they were the only source of support for their mothers. One mother had tuberculosis and no longer had the strength to pick banana leaves and carry them the twelve miles to her village to sell them. The other mother was too malnourished to do anything except beg. After considerable discussion with the charity on how to resolve the problem, I decided to ignore the boys' further education and place them straight into the training unit, so that in a year's time they would have a trade. In the meantime, I arranged a monthly grant for the mothers. This might at first glance appear an obvious solution but I had to be careful not to encourage others in thinking that 'if I threaten to take my child away I will be given cash as well as having him looked after'. Tragically, this kind of blackmail is not uncommon, but I felt a responsibility to my donors to make sure that it didn't happen.

During those early visits, although much of my time was spent dealing with business and financial issues, my real desire was to spend as much time as possible with the children. Being involved in their games and activities, watching them blossom and respond to love, and giving them a feeling of worth was exhilarating. I came to realise how much sponsorship meant to them. The delight on their faces when they received letters and photographs from their sponsors was a joy to see. It wasn't long before the sponsorships spilt over into a newly formed Girls' Home in Trivandrum run by the same charity. The situation for girls was similar to that of the boys except that the only option for the majority of slum girls who didn't marry was a life of prostitution.

Jumping ahead six years into the work, I became increasingly aware there was a great need for clothes. Most of the children wore scanty rags and ran about in bare feet. The latter was resolved by employing a shoemaker who made sandals in leather for 35p a pair. I also noticed a curious fact; if the girls wore school uniforms they were left untouched by the predatory pimps who were always on the prowl for fresh young victims. As I gave talks on the work to groups in and around Norfolk, I was often offered children's clothes. Before long, I was travelling to India with boxes of school uniforms, t-shirts and children's underwear. With the help of a contact at Norwich City Football Club, I persuaded their Training Centre to part with all their out-of-date training kits. The socks, shorts and shirts were too large for the younger children but they were a big hit with the older boys. And when the clothes were too big, they just rolled up the extra length and wore them anyway. (At this time, I was blessed by the services of a company in Thetford, called 'Air Sea and Land', which packaged the clothes for me and shipped them to India.) It was a strange sight to see dozens of Indian boys in the yellow and green strips of Norwich City and little Indian girls in the uniforms of Blofield, Brundall and Hemblington Primary schools, and Norwich and Thorpe High Schools. Sadly, after four large shipments this had to stop. We encountered obstruction from the Indian Customs who banned the imports. The only way to surmount this obstacle was to pay bribes and this I have always refused to do.

Chapter 5   The School for Disabled Children

The previous chapter focussed on my work with the Trivandrum and Madurai Boys' Homes, but I now want to return to the school for the disabled in Madurai, which was what had taken me to India in the first place. From my first visit, I had been working with other charities to raise funds for the school. In addition, I took the initiative to find sponsors for the welfare of individual children and, within two years, I had found sponsors for seventeen of them. Sponsors ensured that they were well dressed and educated, but equally important they provided a reassurance to the disabled children that they were loved. The need to be loved is clearly illustrated in the lives of Satiyan and Abdul.

Satiyan was typical of the many thousands of impoverished disabled children who are born into India's underclass of untouchables. She was profoundly deaf and pitifully thin. No one knew her exact age but she was probably about nine years old. The cause of her deafness was unknown and her background gave her little chance of medical treatment. She grew up in the slums where her early life with her father and mother was brief. Her father, presumably because of the pressures of extreme poverty, took to the local brew of *thara* to blur the edges of his existence and to take away his hunger and the shame of not being able to support his family. The family situation became intolerable and, as a result, Satiyan's mother committed suicide, an all too common means for women to escape from the captivity of despair. The father with his drinking problem was unable to cope, so grandmother stepped in to try to support Satiyan and her two siblings and to save them from the streets.

Satiyan was a boarder at the school and had learnt to be self-sufficient but what she desperately needed was love. I adored her from that first visit when she presented me with a garland of flowers. I kissed her and made a sign of 'Thank you'. On all my visits she would cling to my neck longing for affection. Thankfully, my daughter Jo arranged to sponsor her, ensuring that she stayed at the school until she was old enough to leave. What happened to her then? Who knows? Sadly, neither Jo nor I heard of her again. In those early days I often lost touch with children when they grew old enough to leave sponsorship whereas in later years I have tried to maintain contact with our sponsored children wherever possible.

Abdul had a similar tragic background to Satiyan. He was six years old when I first met him. He also was stone deaf and there was nothing to him but skin and bone, but he was exceedingly beautiful with large mournful eyes. His loving nature made him irresistible. I had only to walk into the building and, like an affectionate cat, he sensed I was there. He would come running and throw his arms around me, holding tightly as though he would never let go. I saw family situations like those of Satiyan and Abdul over and over again in the lives of the other children. It was so important not to become immune to their condition and forget how much little gestures of love meant to them.

For me the rebuilding of the school wasn't just a project, it was a personal obsession driven by my love for the children. I participated energetically in a large fundraising effort in East Anglia and within two years our combined efforts had raised the funds we needed. In 1993 I was privileged to be asked to 'turn the sod' for the foundation stone. Completion of the building was in February 1995 and, as I drove with others through the streets of Madurai to attend the inauguration, I felt utter happiness. "I can't believe this is happening," I said to them. "To think five years ago it was just a dream ..."

I stopped talking. I gasped. There in front of me was the school. The size of the building took me by surprise. It was larger than I'd imagined. Having only seen the early stages of the building work, not much more than the footings, I'd always thought it would be quite small. Now, here it was, three storeys high: I burst into tears, choked with emotion. How had we managed to obtain funding for all this? On entering, I was struck by how airy and spacious it was. The designers had created an atrium that soared through the floors to a glass roof, allowing light in everywhere. There was a proper kitchen: a proper eating hall: proper toilet facilities: and each class had its own room. The place was a hive of activity and the joy on the faces of the children was heart-warming to see.

The opening ceremony was a grand affair with the Collector of Madurai-- equivalent to our mayor—and local and national dignitaries. A platform, covered with an abundance of streamers, had been built, complete with microphones, chairs, fans and sunshades for the important officials. All was perfect but for the one thing. I was saddened that while the 'important people' sat in comfort, the children sat on the open sandy ground in the heat of the glaring sun. For a project organised and run by Christian groups, it did not seem quite right.

This was all still quite new to me but over the years I have found it increasingly difficult to sit on platforms listening to long speeches of self-aggrandisement, while the children I love have to sit on the dusty ground under the beating sun. I now avoid such situations wherever possible or, if I cannot, I join the children after my speech, a policy that has not endeared me to many of the dignitaries. For that opening, I had learnt my first Tamil speech (the result of tuition in Norwich) but the most memorable event of the day was the display of singing and dancing by the children.

In those early years, I spent many happy hours at the school but eventually things began to change. The school's local management decided to transform the school from a free school for disabled children from the slums, to a fee-paying one. We obviously wished for the school to remain unchanged, but our charity was not the biggest donor and our views did not prevail. Fortunately, I was able to arrange for the sponsorship of the seventeen children we were supporting so that they could stay at the school until their leaving age. After that I ceased my involvement.

This was the time that the realisation hit home that working with other organisations and channelling funds through them did not give me or the donors I was representing as much of a say or input in final outcomes as we would have wished. Although I would continue working with other organisations for a year or so—all part of the necessary learning curve—it became obvious that working independently would be the ideal.

Chapter 6   A New Level of Commitment

The visit in 1993 to 'turn the sod' at the school was my fourth to India and was something of a watershed. Until that point I had been visiting India for about a couple of weeks once a year and always as part of the same team. But things had changed. I now had a group of supporters, mainly in Norfolk, who were funnelling funds through me and I felt that I had to be more personally accountable to them. This meant that I had to gain a much more detailed understanding of how the funds were being distributed and, where necessary, to have more influence on the way in which they were used. It was clear that, if the scope of my work and those helping me was to expand, I needed to spend more time in India.

This need for accountability was reinforced at a personal level by an overpowering feeling that, although I had made a difference in the lives of some children, there were so many more that I could help. The memory of that meeting with the dying boy, who shared my drink on a dusty road between Trivandrum and Madurai, never left me. It was as though I saw his shadow in every child I met. Finally, all that I had seen and done to that point gave me confidence that I could accomplish more—that I was not being swept away by unrealistic dreams.

To find out more about what could be done to help these children I spent time with other charities in Bombay (now Mumbai) and Madras (now Chennai). In Bombay I spent a day on an ambulance that went to find sick children on the streets. Sadly, we also found the bodies of two children. It was an invaluable learning time and interesting to see the contrast between small independent charities working on a shoestring and the larger international charities.

What I was going to do on these extended visits was not at first clear to me. I had concerns about some of the groups I was working with, but would it be right to try and work independently of them? If it would, how would I do it? I decided that the best way to start would be simply to spend more time with the children and try to understand their lives and their culture in greater depth. It seems naïve to say it now but I felt that just valuing the children and showing they mattered was justification enough for going. St Francis of Assisi's advice, "Spread the love of God throughout the world and, if necessary, use words" summed up my feelings exactly.

While I had this enormously strong feeling that I had to do more in India, I wondered if I would be doing the right thing for my family. Making longer and more frequent visits would inevitably have a great impact on my daughters, Jo and Claire, who were sixteen and seventeen at the time, and Brian who was about to take early retirement. We sat together one evening at the dinner table to share our thoughts. Brian, Jo and Claire were unanimous in their agreement that I should go for longer periods and gave me their full support. By this time, both my girls had first-hand experience of the work. Claire, as a fourteen-year-old, had accompanied me on my second visit and bonded well with the children. Jo also had built up a real rapport with the boys and girls when she came with me. She would go on to make five more very supportive visits before taking time out to have my grandchildren. She plans to continue her visits when her children are older.

The decision to make more frequent and longer visits moved my involvement with India up to a different level. Had I known that it was to lead to so many disappointments, fears, illnesses, and loneliness, would I have thought differently? Maybe I would have convinced myself that the work already accomplished with the boys' homes and the school for the disabled was enough. I know there were some people who felt that giving up my job and selling my car to enable me to make these extended visits was not the right thing to do for my family. But looking back over twenty years and forty plus visits later, and seeing how much we have been able to accomplish with the backing of so many interested friends and donors, I know that the decision was right—and, more importantly, so do all of my family

So, the extended visits and my street apprenticeship began. In Madurai, I developed a routine: I went to the Boys' Home in the morning, and after the boys had left for school, I walked into the centre of Madurai. I concentrated on a small area of the city visiting the rubbish tips where the slum children were working. Initially they were suspicious. Some threw stones at me, but gradually they became used to me. I would buy some Pepsi Colas and we would gather round for a chat. It doesn't seem much now but it was an initiation, an important part of gaining the acceptance and trust of the children: the groundwork for the bigger things that were to happen later. I learnt a great deal from those hundreds of hours on the streets.

As soon as I arrived back in Norfolk after a visit, I would start seeking ways to finance the next. I took numerous part-time jobs. I washed glasses in a restaurant (Indian, of course), cleaned everything from people's homes to the Municipal toilets, and worked in the day as a home carer and at night as a care assistant. Eventually, I managed to find work participating in the NVQ training of employees in nursing homes. My home parish in Brundall, realising the financial struggle, generously funded a post at the church for ten hours a week for me, flexible enough to fit my trips around it.

I was spurred on by my religious faith that I was doing the right thing and I am convinced that I did benefit from time to time from some real miracles. One of the most unexpected came on one of my early trips. I had set off with a very small amount of personal cash and, as I sat in the Heathrow departure lounge, I worried about how long it would last. Out of the blue, a man came up to me and said: "I don't know who you are or why I am doing it but I know that I have to give you this". He thrust an envelope in my hand and walked away. I opened the envelope and saw that it contained £80—almost double the money I had brought. By this time the man had disappeared into the crowds and, although I searched, I wasn't able to thank him or find out who he was.

Chapter 7   Children of the Streets

By now I had completed several longer visits. Travelling on a low budget meant that staying in even a simple tourist hotel was out of the question. And, even if I could afford to spend £60 a night, would it be right to do so when the children I was trying to befriend only earned 30p a day? In Trivandrum, I accepted the offer of a room in the host charity's building. It was on the top floor up seven flights of stairs. Under the poorly insulated asphalt roof, the heat regularly reached 50 degrees centigrade (over 120 degrees Fahrenheit)— bearable when the fan was working but intolerable during the frequent power cuts. It cost £7 a week. Opening the windows let in some air, but it also let in the mosquitoes. There was a bathroom, but usually no running water, which meant going downstairs to fetch it. As I carried buckets of water up those seven flights of stairs, I thought of the many burdens endured day after day after day by the women in the slums. Because of the shortage of water, I tended to rely on cans of coke to quench my thirst. One day during a power cut, I opened a can of coke but after a few gulps I put it down on the window ledge while I went to try and cool off in the bathroom. I splashed water on myself and then went to finish my drink. I took a big gulp from the can and got a mouthful of coke and lots of gritty bits. I spat it out and, to my horror, saw that the gritty bits were actually red ants! To make matters worse, this was my last drink and so I had nothing to rinse out my mouth. I continued spitting for several hours. Despite the hardships, I made quite a little home out of this room with my indispensable travel kettle acting as a reminder of the comfortable life I'd left behind in the UK.

In Madurai, my accommodation was even more basic. It was a shack in the grounds of the Boys' Home compound close to the local slum and next-door to the village temple. (It was here that I realised how important loud music is to the frequent days-long Hindu festivals!) The shack had concrete walls, a thatched roof, rush matting on the mud floor and a small shower-cum-toilet room. To wash I would stand under the shower while the boys emptied buckets of water into the holding tank above. One shower meant three boys and three buckets of water. The shack had no cooking facilities so I relied on the housemother to make scrambled eggs every morning. The rest of my food came from the city when I was street visiting.

The shack did not have a fan but I was not alone as I struggled with the heat. Frogs, lizards, spiders and cockroaches were always crawling under the matting and, as the walls and the roof did not meet, I was plagued by mosquitoes. I did, however, have access to one electric plug and so, power permitting, I was able to make cups of tea. The conditions in this accommodation would lead directly to the illness that almost killed me and might have ended my work in India. But that was in the future. All I thought about was the thrill of being in India and, once home, earning enough money to enable me to return. These were my two homes for almost four years.

Although I was free to wander the streets of Madurai, the slums were considered too dangerous for a white woman to enter alone. There was considerable wariness about the motivations of foreign visitors. In the past people from Europe and the Middle East had gone into slums, taken photos illustrating the undignified conditions in which people lived, promised to use the photos to raise funds – and then never been seen again. Even worse, I heard of foreign visitors who had befriended children and then sexually abused them, and others who had been instrumental in persuading parents of older children to sell their kidneys for transplant. Not being able to enter the slum was a big disappointment to me, as this was where most of the street children I was meeting every day lived—children whose faces were marked by the miserable conditions of their lives. The face could be that:

> .. of the ten-year-old girl who attempted suicide by dousing herself with kerosene and lighting it. From her chin to her groin was a mass of charred flesh and blisters with scar tissue that restricted her neck muscles. Not for her skin grafts and plastic surgery or antibiotics that would clear any infection. Her mother had no money to pay for a doctor or any form of medical care; all she could do was treat the wounds with crushed tamarind seeds. How many hours, how many days she had lain holding a blanket up to her daughter's neck to keep the flies away from her burns was anyone's guess. Apart from her mother no one cared whether the girl lived or died.

.. of Pitchiamani. He was the first of the three children born to his parents to survive. His birthplace was a pavement in Madurai where his mother earned a meagre living by selling peanuts. His father was dead from heart failure. Pitchiamani was born with his feet twisted and he walked on the outside of his soles, careful to keep a toe in the air for balance. A small operation could have corrected the deformity but it was beyond the means of his mother who barely earned enough for them to survive. By day, he picked up rags in the streets; by night, he ran wild with the other children.

.. of two brothers whose father was a rickshaw puller. Their mother, when new to the slum, argued with some of the older influential residents over water allocation from the slum well. (It was customary for the best 'top' water to go to the senior people in the slum and the sludge waste to the newest arrivals.) She died two days later, supposedly having committed suicide by dousing herself in kerosene and setting it alight. The father could not look after the boys as well as work so the two brothers roamed the streets.

.. of Mutiah. He was about thirteen years old. He was more fortunate than the other children as he had paid work. His job was to go down the manholes into the sewers and sift through the sand, silt and effluent for scrap metal. His dream was to find gold. More likely, he would find injury and disease. He might even find death, drowning in a flash flood, as water poured through the sewers in the rainy season.

.. of the young girl, no more than a child, carrying her new-born baby conceived through prostitution. The umbilical cord of the baby was infected. Already the mother of two other young children who were both deaf and infested with lice, she refused even the little help she was offered, fearing that if she left the security of the small shack she shared with another family of beggars she would never be able to return.

.. of Ayyaner. He was about four years old. His mother was dead and his father had abandoned him when he remarried. Ayyaner wandered from shack to shack in the slum begging for food. In one ankle he had a deeply infected wound that was alive with maggots. One day I carried

51

him to a private clinic for treatment but was turned away because he was an untouchable.

.. of a seven-year-old boy whose stepmother didn't want him. Every time he went home, she burnt him with a cigarette. He roamed the streets and had discovered that if he allowed himself to be abused once or twice a week he could earn enough money for food.

So many children but one face - the face of despair and hopelessness.

The plight of the street children weighed heavily on my heart—anonymous children, ground down by poverty. Children as young as four begging or working in pitiful conditions for just a few rupees. There are no precise figures of how many such children there are: one estimate is that there are 28,000 of them in Madurai alone. The figures will be much higher in the bigger cities like Chennai and Mumbai.

So, where do these children come from? Who are they? Most come from the slums—untouchables shunned and despised by many of their fellow countrymen. They suffer from a variety of medical problems; many are born with a disability. Often the children of a single parent, unable to work through ill health, they roam the streets begging or working to provide income for their families. Some children live alone, having run away to escape beatings, family breakdown, and extremes of poverty that we in the West find difficult to comprehend. Some are orphans, whose parents have died of disease or malnutrition. Others have been abandoned by mothers who cannot look after them. Some children are sold into bonded labour usually as Hotel Workers. Although some of these live in squalid accommodation provided by their employer, there are many who roam the streets sleeping rough. Others make their home in places where, for a piece of floor and occasional food, they will be overworked, abused and ill-treated.

When they reach puberty some boys and many girls turn to prostitution, falling into the clutches of pimps who prowl the streets, always on the lookout for fresh young bodies. Fortunately, over the years, things have improved. More girls are attending college and wearing a school uniform seems to offer some protection. Nevertheless, sexually-transmitted infections are increasing;

HIV/AIDS has become a serious problem because of poor medical hygiene. Some children turn to drug trafficking or begging but the majority of street children become rag-pickers, spending their days looking for rags and pieces of scrap metal in the open sewers that flow through the slums. There was an apathy about them that I found distressing; when I asked one boy if he would be part of a programme that would allow him and some other children to attend school, he looked at me with an air of resignation and sadness and said "Patamma, [Pat-mother] it is as it is". How many times would I hear similar words?

In India, there is little or no organised system of waste collection and rubbish is literally thrown into the streets. A few sweepers, untouchables, receive a token payment from the Government to keep the streets reasonably clean but most of their income derives from picking over the rubbish they collect. They sweep and create piles of rubbish--food waste, paper, cloth, metal scrap, shredded tyres—stinking heaps where cows, oxen, goats, dogs and humans defecate; homes to rats, cockroaches and mosquitoes. The rag pickers spend their days in places like these, picking over the waste, separating the elements and selling the bundles to middlemen who sell it on for re-cycling. They are exposed to virulent infectious diseases which quickly spread from person to person. In addition they run the risk of being robbed, especially the children. Rag-pickers earn about 60 pence in a fourteen to sixteen hour day, depending on the quality of the rubbish.

The demand for people to do the filthy menial tasks that no one else wants to do underpins the status of the untouchable and frustrates attempts to abolish the caste system. The Government periodically rounds up street children and places them in centres which provide an education. Unfortunately, this sometimes causes other problems as many families depend on the earnings of their children for survival. And, difficult as home life is, some children run away from the centres rather than give up the freedom they find on the streets. Various religious and secular organisations run worthy projects to aid street children but these only scratch the surface because it is so difficult to address the underlying problem of general poverty.

There are no quick solutions and over time I have come to realise that abolishing child labour cannot happen overnight. Without the child's income the family starves. Any attempt to abolish child labour has to go hand in hand with raising family incomes above subsistence level. A planned programme of part-time education and better working conditions is likely to be more successful than outright abolition. Children's Homes and Orphanages offer a secure haven for a few, but thousands of children live on the streets, unloved and uneducated.

Spending all my spare time wandering the streets talking to the children seemed so inadequate but I could think of little else to do. As I came to know some of them by name, I became bolder and invited them to meet me at a central open space in the evening, where we enjoyed biscuits, drinks, singsongs and games of cricket—anything to break the treadmill drudgery of their lives for a brief moment before they returned to work next day. When I reflect on my approach now, it seems naïve, yet all I could do was surround myself with these lovely kids who only asked for affection and time to be children. The worst crime of all for me is when the children are not valued as individuals. Many in the higher castes regard them as vermin. Whenever I encounter street children, I am struck by the sadness in their eyes and the despair that hangs about them; yet how quickly that can change when I smile at them and show them recognition. I have seen a morose, emaciated boy brought into one of our sponsored homes transformed into a vibrant and intelligent child, merely by being loved and cared for. It is heart-warming to see the transformation into children overflowing with mischief and fun and bursting with the exuberance of living.

As my visits to India increased, the desire to do more for these children grew. I recognised that those working in the homes were doing a good job in providing for the children's physical needs but I became increasingly convinced that more needed to be done for their spiritual needs. Providing food and a safe place to sleep was essential for the children's physical growth but spiritual growth required the giving of genuine affection, love and respect. I shared my ideas with some of the workers and they at first looked a little concerned. They feared that 'providing spiritual needs' was a euphemism for conversion to Christianity; a practice still frowned upon in India and, indeed, forbidden until a few years ago. To put their minds at rest, I hastily added, "By spiritual needs, I'm referring to the part of us that responds to love, praise, and respect. Our physical wellbeing is vital but equally important is the wellbeing that comes from being loved." It was a good discussion and I could see one or two agreed with what I was trying to say. Later, over a breakfast discussion, I told them about my get-togethers with children on the nearby open waste ground. "One thing we could do for the children would be to find a proper meeting place with a roof and a kitchen facility." "I know just the place," one of the workers said and later that day took me to a ramshackle building, that was cheap to rent and conveniently situated near the slum. We snapped it up.

On the opening day of the drop-in centre, fifty filthy, boisterous, wonderful boys attended. They were difficult to control but responsive. Everyone was a joy to be with. It was a day of laughter, fun, tears, tragic stories and lots of love. As I went to bed that night I was shattered, but neither my exhaustion nor the scabies and head lice I had picked up diminished the elation I felt about this significant breakthrough and the many new friends I had made.

Mum and Dad

Working with Sid James

Me as a baby

At the holiday camp

A map of India showing where our work is being carried out

Original boys' home, 1991

This is me with Balamuragan at the Madurai boys' home. He went on to found a successful paint business.

Madurai slum 1994

Madurai slum 2012

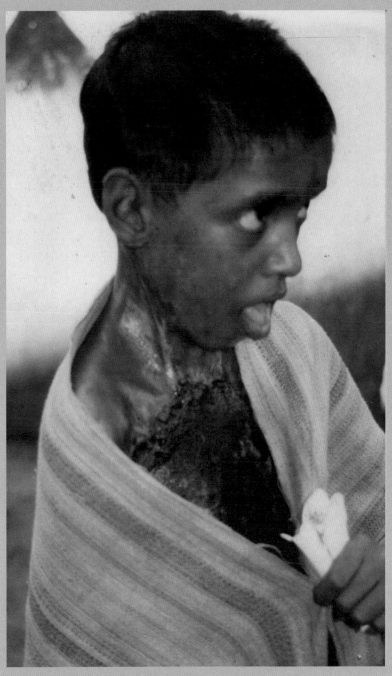

One of my most painful memories is of this young girl who tried
to commit suicide (page 50)

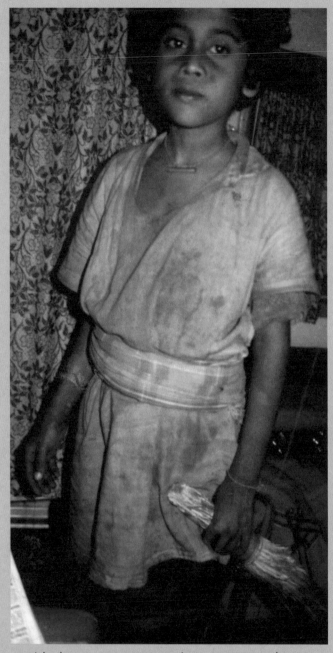

A street girl who came onto my train to sweep up the mouse and rat droppings (page 89)

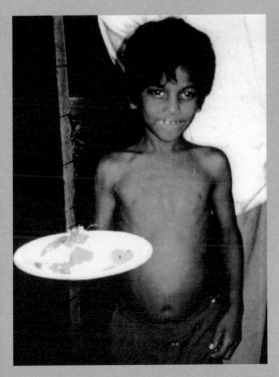

A boy pleased with his food at our first camp (page 87)

Hotel boys relaxing at the drop-in centre (page 100)

My daughters Claire and Jo in India

The boys' home where I had my hut

With the ambulance outside the Regional Cancer Centre

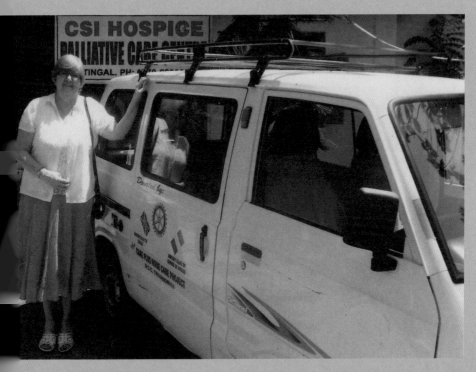

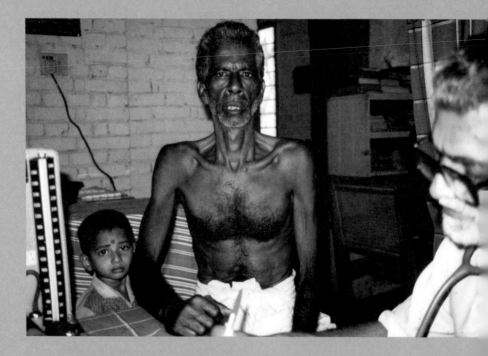

Cancer patient

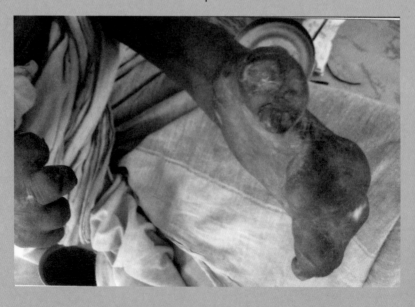

The effects of leprosy on one of our ladies

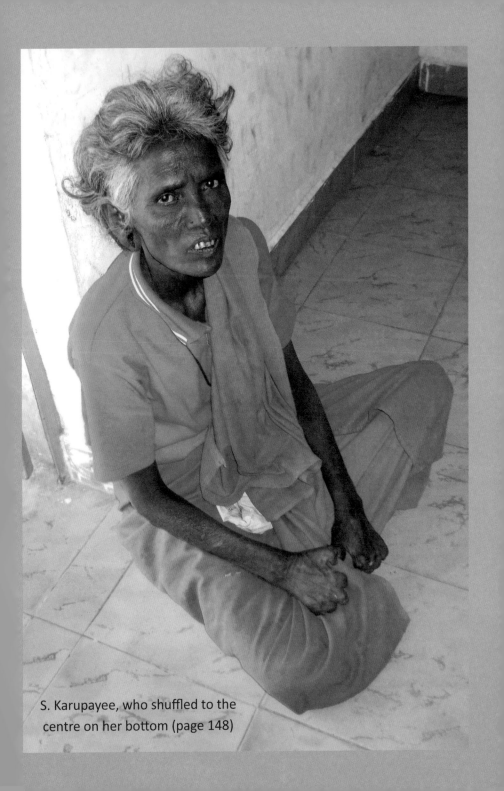

S. Karupayee, who shuffled to the centre on her bottom (page 148)

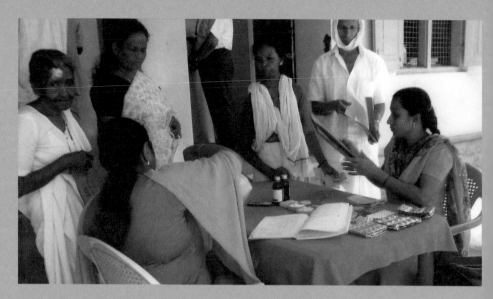

One of our cancer clinics

On a home visit with Shoba

Meenakshi delivering food to a pilgrim travelling "without purse or scrip."

Jacob-Thomas, the first boy I sponsored, now married with a child and working as a carpenter. In this picture he is making holding crosses for distribution in the UK. (page 150)

Jacob and Jesse

Education centre at Mavelikara funded by the Norwich diocese. The complex also includes a boys' home and a girls' home. (page 134)

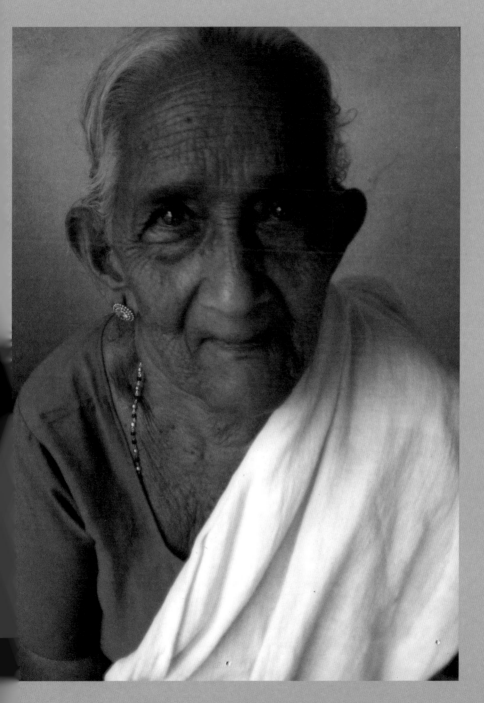

Janaki, one of the Mavelikara grannies

Mavelikara grannies wearing the saris that they requested to show they belong to our project (page 136)

One of the boys who moved from the Trivandrum home to Mavelikara

Chapter 8   Entering the Slum

Still excited by the success of the opening night at the drop-in centre, I met up with some of the workers from the charity the following day. They had invited me to accompany them to photograph some of the areas around the slum. As we moved towards the slum one of them landed me with a bombshell. "Pat, why not come into the slum itself?" I stood there speechless. The silence on my part was the shock of being asked. I could not believe I'd heard correctly. They were inviting me to enter the place where, for the last three years, I'd been advised never to venture. I knew the slum dwellers were deeply suspicious of Westerners. Many of the foreigners who had gone into the slums over the years had either misled or disappointed the people. They had raised hopes with ambitious projects and then dashed them again by disappearing with the funding in their own pockets.

Some children had been taken away for kidney harvesting. A man comes to a woman of the slum and says, "I am a surgeon. You have a healthy son. He doesn't need both kidneys. I'll pay you £200 for one of them." With a husband unable to work and fears that her daughters will end up as prostitutes, she is easily persuaded. £200 will keep the family from starvation for at least two years. Botched operations mean that some boys are never well again. All these things have engendered a total mistrust of foreigners and their motives.

"Pat, why not come into the slum itself?" The question was repeated. This time, without hesitation, I answered, "Yes". With two of the charity workers, I walked to the edge of the slum. As we stood in the road, there were some very suspicious looks even though my colleagues were well-known in the area. I cannot say what my expectations were. But despite my experience of seeing people living in shacks we wouldn't keep a dog in, people sleeping in doorways and trying to exist on almost no money, nothing had prepared me for what I saw that day. This slum in Madurai had no specific boundaries but was nevertheless well defined. It was set back off the highway and access to it was by three paths between the shacks that lined the road. The background canvas of the slum was a lifeless mixture of dark brown, grey and black that merged into a dull muddy monochrome. My first impression was of a still-life picture with the colour brushed out, but then my eye would catch the splash of red of a water pot and I would be aware of movement and noise. The centre of the slum was a square of tenement buildings six to eight storeys high. The outer wall of one block had collapsed and the building looked as if it could topple at any moment.

Around the centre, spreading outwards, were hundreds of small makeshift shacks made from old corrugated iron sheeting, pallet boards, bricks of baked cow dung, cardboard and other scrap material. Open sewers ran alongside the shacks draining into large pits at the back of the slum. In these squalid ramshackle hovels lived hundreds of families and in each one a mother attempted to make a home. Effluent bubbled up through the ground from the sewers and lapped the concrete slabs that made the walkways. Naked children splashed and played in stinking puddles of stagnant water. There were two toilets for the whole slum: human and animal excrement was everywhere. There were few water pumps and the water was only turned on for short periods each day. Pigs, goats, cows and chickens roamed freely. Rats, fleas and cockroaches were everywhere. Most dangerous of all were the dogs that prowled among the huts; any one of them could be carrying rabies. The sewage pits were breeding grounds for millions of mosquitoes that multiplied in the rainy season and carried the waterborne diseases of malaria, typhoid and numerous infections known only to the inhabitants as 'fevers'.

The spicy smell from the cooking pots on the many open fires could not mask the stench of rotting sewage which impregnated everything in the slum. My companions drew me in a little further and then briefed me to wait until they gave me the signal to move forward. That was the plan, but as I stood there I made eye contact with a thin young woman who looked about thirty but who was probably much younger. She had striking long dark hair tied back with a parting down the middle. I particularly noticed her badly misshapen feet covered in sores. Around her eyes were the usual flies. On her hip she was carrying a naked baby about ten months old, who looked surprisingly fit and well. She smiled. Spontaneously I moved forward, held out my hand and smiled back. She just nodded and the baby's little hands reached out trying to touch my face. I moved a little nearer. The baby gave the broadest grin, squealed with delight and strained towards me even more, begging me to carry him. Instinctively, I held out my arms and he leapt into them.

It was a magical moment that totally changed the atmosphere around us. The invisible barriers came down. People began to smile and laugh and a crowd gathered round us. We were no longer strangers from different cultures; we were just two women enjoying the antics of a small baby. And I sensed this was the moment. "Start walking," a voice inside me said. Carrying the baby, I walked into the heart of the slum, with the woman beside me. I smiled at those around me. The baby beamed and gurgled with delight. I must have hesitated for a moment afraid we were going too far but the others behind me whispered in my ear, "Just keep going. Don't stop."

Children, many I already knew, started running out of the shacks and the rag shops, laughing and shouting, "Patamma, Patamma." As they crowded around me, some of the adults joined them and it soon became a carnival. All those years of work and here I was at last. I could hear mutterings in the crowd, "Who is she? Who is she?" and the children shouting out my name. As I walked deeper and deeper into the slum I was overcome with happiness. I wanted to sit down and cry out of sheer elation. In this place of indescribable squalor, filth and overpowering smells, surrounded by dozens of children and holding another mother's baby in my arms, I had a glimpse of heaven. A ridiculous thought I suppose, but it was the most amazing, wonderful, humbling, incredible feeling. It may seem a strange thing to say and even harder to believe but, despite all the filth and misery, this slum was where I wanted to be and where I felt most at home when I was in India. Because it was here I came to know some of the bravest and loveliest people I have ever met: people who, day after day, picked rags in the sewer hoping to bring in enough money to survive; people who endured an endless grind to stay alive.

Health problems abounded. Most common were worm infestations, scabies, head lice, open infected wounds, weeping eyes, chicken pox and asthma. At that time, there were thirty-five deaths a month from rabies in the city slums and surrounding area. Typhoid, with its symptoms of aching limbs, headaches, diarrhoea and vomiting, broke out in four to five year cycles resulting in hundreds of deaths.

There are some images that will never leave me—the shrivelled old lady covered in sores, and probably dying, whose daughter caught my arm and asked me to pray for her mother. Sadly, I had no miraculous powers to bring healing but I hope I was able to give some comfort by praying with them. The next day, I took her some steamed rice cakes, paste and plantains. Although she could barely move, she turned on her side and crammed the food into her mouth. Before I left I hugged her and the gratitude in her eyes taught me how much one small act of kindness can mean. If we all helped just one person at a time, it would change the world.

I shall never forget sitting on a 'porch' in the middle of the slum telling stories to a boisterous crowd of children when suddenly the air was filled with smoke, followed by a few seconds of terrible screaming and then an awful smell of cooked meat. A seventy-year old man had poured kerosene over himself and set it alight. The tragedy, which left me deeply shaken, caused a stir for a few minutes but then life carried on as if nothing had happened. The children seemed wholly unaffected as though it was the most normal thing in the world. Sadly, it was not unusual. There were approximately five suicides a month in the slum. The old man may have been starving or in pain. He may have recognised the onset of rabies or advanced tuberculosis. Whatever the cause, he had wanted to escape from the misery of his existence. The casualness of it all horrified me. All I could do was say a prayer for him.

After my first visit, I was pleased at how quickly I won the people's trust. As I visited the slum over the years, I forged many close relationships. Of course, the children helped a lot. Even those I did not know would cluster round me and I was constantly having babies thrust into my arms and being asked to kiss them. Saying that I loved being there in the slum does not mean that I was not nervous and horrified at what I saw. It was terrifying that people were condemned to live in conditions such as these, but exciting to see that in the apparent hopelessness there were those who could still smile. At heart, they were no different from families everywhere, struggling to bring up their children to a better life, to find happiness, to be loved.

An unexpected bonus of my visits to the slum was my growing friendship with the old women. Deeply lined faces, desperately thin bodies, but what beautiful toothless grins they gave when they were shown affection. Underneath the squalor there was a vast sea of love. Later, I organised some picnic lunches for these elderly women; they were overjoyed by these rare chances to relate to one another in a relaxed social atmosphere. I did not expect a similar response from the men. Elderly Hindu men do not approach any woman, let alone a Westerner - but there was one old man, grey hair, sparkling eyes, who always smiled when I passed. One day I boldly approached him with the typical hands-together greeting. As I left he hugged me. Others went out of their way to shake my hand.

The condition of the sick elderly slum-dwellers was pitiful. They sat or lay almost motionless, as if glued to their spot. They knew that if they left their patch to get food or to go to hospital for treatment, it would probably be taken before they got back. Sadly, this slum was only one of many. Similar slums could be found all over the country. My work eventually moved to another slum, but that slum and those wonderful people will always remain in my heart.

On one occasion, Jacob, one of the workers to whom I felt particularly close, took me into another slum, this time in Trivandrum city. It was home to several hotel maids, one of whom—a lady who cleaned the toilets—I had met before and become particularly fond of. I became so absorbed in the quest to find her that I didn't notice that Jacob and I had become separated. To my delight, I found the lady. She was very pleased to see me and at once invited me to her home, where she offered me a drink of fizzy orange. Bottles of pop were safe to drink and, not wanting to spurn her hospitality, I thanked her and began to drink. I was very thirsty and had already taken several big gulps when a stricken Jacob rushed up to me and screamed at me to stop. He told me that what I had thought was orange pop was, in fact, stagnant well water flavoured with orange powder. I thanked the lady and said goodbye quickly. What happened next still makes me laugh to recall. In a state of panic, I decided to retroactively purify the bad water. I swiftly crammed two water purifying tablets into my mouth, washed them down with some safe bottled water and then spent the next couple of hours jumping up and down. I hoped that the pills would mix with the well water in my stomach and kill the bacteria before they got absorbed into my blood stream. It worked!

Happily this slum is no more. In 2009 the Indian Government bulldozed it and filled in the open sewers. The inhabitants were granted a payment by the Government that was sufficient to allow them to build rather better accommodation in a new community.

Chapter 9   The Frail and the Sick

It was an Indian doctor—a truly Good Samaritan—who first helped me to understand what it means to be frail and sick in the slums. On one of my early visits he invited me to his home for a delightful dinner, cooked by his charming wife, and told me how he had begun his slum medical centre. "I had been visiting a friend," he recalled, "and was driving home along National Highway 47 when I saw an old couple. The old man was bent double under the weight of his wife. He was finding it difficult to keep her from falling as her grip around his neck was failing. I drove by but the further I went the more the parable of the Good Samaritan nagged at me. So much so, that in the end I turned the car round and drove back to them. The man told me he was taking his wife to the Government Hospital thirty miles from his village. I could see his wife was very sick and probably dying. I feared he would never make it so I helped them into the car and took them the rest of the way. As I left, I gave them some money and said I'd pay more if needed."

The village was in a poor drought stricken rural area of about forty square miles and home to 500,000 people. There were no medical care facilities, and even if there had been, the people would not have had the money to pay for them. Most of the inhabitants relied on the local farms for employment but there was only enough work for two to three days a week, so survival was dependent upon what they could grow in their own gardens. The available work was shared among the villagers producing a weekly income just enough to feed a whole family. Working in this searing hot climate had an adverse effect on their health.

"I returned two days later on hospital business," the doctor continued, "and discovered the old lady had died. The man had left and was walking the thirty-mile journey back to his village. I jumped in the car and drove after him hoping to find him. I eventually caught up with him, trudging along the highway in the choking dust and heat. I picked him up and drove him the rest of the way home. I was so overcome by the conditions the people lived in that

I felt driven to do something to improve them." That 'something' was to form a Society with a number of friends and build a clinic near the village.

The doctor and his friends were all part of the local Christian community who had found inspiration from Jesus' words, "Whatever you do for one of the least of these brothers of mine, you do for me." A legacy of £12,000 from one of the members had enabled them to build a rudimentary building and to offer virtually free treatment, and the clinic became a shining light of Christian service to desperately poor people. For those of us in Britain where our National Health Service, despite its shortcomings, offers a high standard of medical attention for all, it's hard to imagine that in so many countries even the most basic treatment is only available to those who can pay for it.

Life expectancy in poor Indian communities is below fifty years. Diseases that we have almost eradicated in the UK are commonplace. People die by the hundred every day from tuberculosis, tetanus, leprosy, malnutrition, skin diseases, amoebic dysentery, asthma and many other complaints that are untreatable without the right medication or surgery. Poor sanitation and lack of water cause parasitic infections. One that is endemic and no respecter of persons is Scabies, caused by a mite that burrows into the skin and lays its eggs usually between the fingers or the buttocks, or in the armpits. The symptoms are a rash and intense itching. It is not life threatening but most unpleasant and acquired through contact. I know it well!

The worst affliction is worm infestation: hookworm: roundworm: pinworm: take your pick. The cause is, again, a lack of sanitation in overcrowded conditions. Worms leave the body through the motions and, since faecal matter goes directly into the soil used for planting crops, an invidious cycle begins. The symptoms are itching in the rectum, irritability and, in the case of roundworm, indigestion and sometimes a cough. In severe cases worms cause anaemia in which the red area inside the lower eyelid loses its colour. If untreated, the worms cause severe pain as they enter the lungs or cause intestinal blockages. They can reach a considerable size in the adult stage and are sometimes expelled live through vomiting. With modern medication, de-worming is relatively straightforward, but in India modern medicines are not readily available to the poor. Unfortunately, even if treated, the results are invariably short-lived as re-infestation is almost inevitable. The Government Health Service is struggling against a tide of poverty and an increasing population. The few state hospitals lack a nursing service. Each patient has a metal bed with no bedding in an overcrowded ward with little or no ventilation. Members of the family are expected to cook the patient's food on the little stoves provided. Patients who want water when there is no family member available have to pay.

In Indian culture there is a committed sense of family that acts as the support unit in the absence of a Welfare State. The traditional family structure is that the woman joins her husband's household on marriage and comes to live in the family home—a system that can work reasonably well for parents who have sons. There is, and always was, an expectation that parents are cared for in their old age by their children. This worked reasonably well when Indian society was static, but, as India develops, increasing mobility is becoming the norm and children have begun to move away from their parents to different parts of India and to other countries. The resulting break-up of traditional family life brings much unhappiness. Despite Government attempts to tackle the overwhelming effects of poverty, very little is done for the elderly. There is no fall-back provision for them if they are not cared for by their families. The situation is even more acute for untouchables. Many are so desperately poor that they cannot afford to feed and clothe their children. The many who fall outside the family safety net gather what they can by working or begging.

In some hospitals treatment is provided free by fine dedicated doctors but the lack of nursing aftercare means poor hygiene. I have witnessed drips crawling with maggots and in one intensive care unit I saw rats running about. The Government does not intend it to be like this but the service is swamped by the sheer weight of numbers. Private hospitals exist where the quality of healthcare depends upon what patients can pay. Sadly, corruption distorts the effectiveness of some of these hospitals. I have heard stories of unneeded drugs being prescribed and hospital stays needlessly prolonged. I saw the problems of one private hospital in the family of one of our workers. His eldest son, normally a boisterous lad, had become lethargic, and was even falling asleep at school. A private doctor diagnosed a brain tumour and advised expensive and highly risky surgery. His father approached me for help. Calling on my basic nursing training, I examined the boy myself and was convinced that he was suffering from anaemia. Some iron tablets and an improved diet saw a recovery in less than a month. I was to experience for myself the poor quality of care in the private sector in 1996 when I contracted amoebic dysentery. The negligent treatment had severe repercussions on my health and almost meant the end of my work in India...but more of that later.

With the lack of affordable health care in outlying villages, primitive tribal medicine is the only thing available. Hence, the development of the clinic I mentioned earlier was a blessing beyond measure. My involvement with the clinic began in 1992 when the doctor took me to see the work of this small mission. By then the original building had become a small thatched roof, two-roomed hospital about 400 square feet in size. It was built a mile from the outskirts of the village and each day provided basic medical treatment, free of charge, to over one hundred patients who lived within a twenty-mile radius. Close proximity to the people was important as even one day off work could mean a whole family suffering for lack of food. The two highly qualified Indian doctors who ran the hospital were incredible. They worked with dedication and brilliance, totally devoted to what they were doing. Both had given up highly lucrative careers to live and work among the poorest of the poor, working twelve hours a day, six days a week, in blistering heat, because they believed it was where God wanted them to be. I was moved by their fervour and commitment.

The décor and furnishings of the surgery were spartan, consisting of a table and a curtained examination table. Equipment was limited to one sphygmomanometer for measuring blood pressure, one thermometer, and one spatula. Before surgery there was a time of prayer as the doctors prepared themselves for the busy time ahead. Then the doors opened and the patients streamed through two at a time. The absence of confidentiality was not an issue to these thin, desperate people, so grateful for the treatment they received. With so little equipment, assessments were made by touch. The skill of the lady doctor was amazing. She could diagnose with her fingertips and seemed to possess a sixth sense, invariably proved to be right by subsequent test results.

To my surprise the most common problem was asthma. Every other patient, from adults to wheezing children, seemed to suffer from it. The doctors explained that it was caused by the intense dry heat coupled with overcrowding, poor sanitation and malnourishment. All they could do was treat the symptoms. A mournful-looking older lady came in with a pus filled cervical polyp that the doctor had tried to treat with antibiotics. These were not working so he decided to remove it there and then. I found myself monitoring the pulse of this dear soul as the doctor removed the polyp with limited local anaesthesia. Holding that tiny hand in mine, I felt the real spirit of their work and a sense of privilege to be there with them.

Later, I watched the doctor examining ears and throats with no more than an ordinary household torch. None of the patients seemed to object to my being there. Young and old alike, often in pain, would give me friendly smiles. One lady arrived bleeding internally. She had walked twenty miles from her home. I watched this poor woman have an operation with almost no anaesthetic. "I'm horrified at how far that woman had to walk in her condition," I said to the doctor afterwards. "That's what most of them do," he replied. "They know we're qualified doctors and they believe the walk is worth it. The treatment is not only good but it's also free." The last patient of the day was a girl with a severely infected foot. I helped to hold her down while the doctor dug deep with the scalpel to drain pus-filled abscesses on the sole. All this with no anaesthetic. Although the relief for the girl was obvious at the end, the pain she must have experienced sent me reeling. At the end of that one visit, it was clear to me I should ask those supporting me to help. One brief telephone call to the UK assured the hospital of an immediate donation of £1,000 to equip the pharmacy.

Shortly after I returned home, I was sitting in the prayer room at Norwich Cathedral when a thought popped into my mind. "Don't just sit here. They need an ambulance." I left the prayer room and telephoned the treasurer of the clinic. Amazed, I heard him say they'd just finished a prayer meeting where they'd prayed for an ambulance. Within six weeks I had gathered the funds and an ambulance was purchased. The hospital was now able to run clinics at four compass points in that twenty-mile radius, reducing the maximum walking distance for any villager to eight miles. The first journey made by the ambulance was to take a baby who had died of asthma home. Had it not been available, the parents would have had to walk from the hospital to their home village—a distance of several miles—carrying the baby in their arms.

On another occasion, a young boy fell from a tree and sustained severe head injuries. The ambulance was able to get him to a large city hospital in time, thus saving his life. The next purchases, funded by UK colleagues, were a dental chair and equipment plus one year's salary for a dentist. This was a direct consequence of a patient who came to the hospital with an open wound on his cheek, a mixture of blood and pus, the result of an abscess that had eaten through his cheek and jawbone. Before long, the hospital was unable to cope with the ever increasing numbers asking for treatment and soon a dream hospital, financed by the Society, was under way. When completed it had a reception area, a ward, an operating theatre, a delivery room, a dental surgery, and a small dispensary.

The number of patients continued to increase. One day I was there, the ward was overcrowded with fourteen patients, the majority with respiratory problems but others with burns, severe dehydration, a toe amputation and the usual worm infections. Patients arrived in all kinds of transport. On one occasion the village bus made a detour in order to drop a patient at the door. A paediatrician attended twice a week and the average number of patients visiting the clinic each day rose to two hundred. It was a joy to see people relieved of pain, but there were many occasions when I was saddened by the intense suffering of patients. I shall never forget the fourteen-year-old girl brought in with lumps in her armpit. Her father had died two years before of lymph node tuberculosis. A year later her sixteen year old sister had died a painful death in the same way. And now the doctor with tears in her eyes had to confirm the inevitable to the mother. Nor shall I forget the elderly woman who came to the clinic severely infected with tuberculosis. She was very thin with deep sunken eyes. Her efforts to breathe through a hacking cough were an intense struggle. The disease had taken such a hold that there was nothing the doctors could do.

After the clinic, I walked through the village to find her sitting outside her shack trying to catch her breath in the humid heat. She relied on her neighbours to bring her water. Not for her the air-conditioned room, the cool bath, or the feel of soft clean clothes to ease her suffering. Her prognosis was wretched—a slow, painful death huddled on the dust of the floor in her shack. We sat together and I put my arms around her, just skin and bone. She asked me to pray for her and as I did so I wept inside. This incident started me thinking of the possibilities of bringing palliative care, then an unheard of concept, to the village areas. Many years later, in a different context and after forming a new charity, I was able to turn this concept into a reality.

A small hospice was started by the Society soon after. One of the first patients was Maria, found on the street suffering from a mental disability. She had been the victim of severe abuse. She wouldn't talk, showed no sign that she could hear, and made no eye contact. In the hospice she was bathed, her filthy matted hair cut and washed, and dressed in a new sari. I spent short periods with her and it was a joy to hear her laugh for the first time. I gave her a comb and some moisturised wipes as I left, which I noticed she quickly squirreled away out of sight.

I am frequently asked when I speak about India, "What do the Indian people do to help themselves?" Places like this clinic are the answer. The excitement of seeing it all in those early days has still not left me and in no small part dictated my future work in the area of palliative care.

During this period my concern for the elderly on the streets was growing. It came into particularly sharp focus when I met Apou. He had lived in his brother's house but when his brother and sister-in law died the rest of the family threw him out. He tried to work but a chest problem hampered him and he now lived as a vagrant, sleeping in doorways and begging for food. Apou always hung around the smart hotels. He looked about ninety years old but was probably in his early fifties. He was tall with matted white hair and a great bushy white beard down to his stomach. Although thin, he reminded me of a picture book representation of Father Christmas. He used to give me a big beaming smile whenever our paths crossed. At first I only smiled in acknowledgement but before long I began to give him food. I looked forward to seeing him on my visits until one year he was missing. I was concerned and after enquiries discovered he was ill with severe boils and too weak to be at his usual pitch. Once I found him, I persuaded him to have treatment. He was admitted to hospital and speedily cured. After that, whenever he saw me, he would come rushing from his doorway, fall to his knees and try to kiss my feet! On one occasion, he stood up and reached into his pocket for a small packet of neatly folded newspaper. He unwrapped it, took out a fluff-covered sweet and put it into my mouth. I hesitate to think where it had been previously. I sucked it nervously. Spitting it out would have insulted his generosity. The sweet was all he had and his only means of saying thank you. Even now the thought of the love behind the gift makes me well up inside.

His story is an individual one but typical of so many of the elderly living rough. Others like him live in alleyways, doorways or anywhere they can create a small space to sleep. Many are disabled, deformed by leprosy and disfigured by disease. Simple surgery or medicine could remedy many of their ills but, funding apart, few can be persuaded to leave their pitch for possible treatment in hospital, because they are afraid that it will be taken by someone else while they are away. They are generally resigned to their lot in life. The memory of one old lady who lived in the Madurai slum still haunts me. When I saw her, she was lying partly in a pool of stagnant water, her matted hair covered in lice. The missing fingers on her hands were evidence of active advanced leprosy. I tried to arrange for her to move to a shelter of Mother Teresa's but she refused to go. The slum was all she knew. Kindly neighbours were aware of her and gave her a little help. I fed and cleaned her on the day I first met her but, as she would not move, there was little else I could do.

Another moving story involves members of a street family who were begging near my Trivandrum hostel room. The young mother had three children including a boy of about seven. I used to give them food and we offered to take her children into our newly formed homes and to give her work. She did not accept the offer and, on my next visit, I was sad to learn that her seven-year-old son had died of rabies.

Over the years I have become so accustomed to the sights and sounds of the streets and slums, that I sometimes think that nothing can shock me. But then, at an unexpected moment, I'm caught unawares by an incident that moves me to tears. Once, while I was trying to hail an auto rickshaw, an elderly man approached me. He had one leg and supported himself on crutches. In a hurry and not wanting to be distracted, I thrust some money at him but he waved it away. He looked as if he had leprosy, as there were small open cuts all down the front of his leg, one or two through to the bone. Something like gentian violet was painted over them. He grabbed my arm, turned, and showed me the back of his leg that had two large weeping sores. He held a piece of stick, made a shaking movement with it and pointed to one of the sores. I felt sick. It was crawling with maggots. He gestured again with the stick and gave it to me. He wanted me to flick the maggots off. Suddenly, the rush to get a rickshaw seemed less important.

There have been lighter moments like the old woman I found sitting by a well. After a few smiles I offered her a box of cakes I'd just bought. She looked at me suspiciously at first, as though I might be trying to poison her. Tentatively she picked one up and took a bite. Then, throwing caution to the wind, shovelled the rest into her mouth with great relish. With cream all over her face, and to the amusement of the onlookers, she grabbed the box and rushed off to share the rest of the cakes with her friends.

The enthusiasm and concern of the medical Society gave me an idea of how together we might bring relief to some of the elderly. In 1995, we devised a simple project that involved taking food packets onto the streets of Trivandrum on a regular basis. One of the younger members of the Society agreed to head the project. As a pilot exercise, we went out one evening with packets of food, looking for street people who spent the night in the area around the station. We soon came across a starving elderly couple. We gave them a food package and they directed us to a group of twelve elderly lepers nearby. They were ragged and thin, and most had extremities missing; two had lost complete limbs: one man had no hands or feet. He was living in the doorway of a shop. These people had no way of caring for themselves. Most days their only food was the leftovers from the hotels.

It was agreed that the project should continue. The food runs would happen once a week. £5 would provide 50 food packets. By the time I left for home we had made about twenty food runs. In those early days I was inexperienced enough to think they would continue in my absence. Unfortunately, once I returned to the UK, the enthusiasm waned and these particular food runs only took place intermittently.

Sadly, my involvement with the Society ended after the death of the treasurer who had become a dear friend. After he died the ethos began to change. Charges were introduced for some operations and treatments and the original two doctors, unhappy with the new developments, decided to move on. The disappointing end to this project, however, should not take away from the wonderful work accomplished during those early years. Thousands of poor people were treated and their lives saved by inspired and dedicated doctors. The vision which led to the building of the hospital is a glowing example of what can be achieved when a few people put their faith into action. They taught me a lot.

Another hospital link I was able to establish was with a doctor who worked on the Dermatology Ward of the local Government Hospital in Trivandrum. She was twenty-four years old when I first met her, recently graduated and dedicated to working with the poor. Her speciality was leprosy (called Hanson's disease in India because of the stigma of 'leprosy'). She showed me round her ward and introduced me to the drugs available. Many of her patients were in an advanced stage of the disease and the smell of rotting flesh was almost unbearable. "The Government only provides free medicines to treat existing symptoms." she told me. "The infected ulcers are treated either medically or surgically but they are not the underlying cause. Without long-term drug therapy the symptoms return within weeks." I asked how long the drug therapy took. "About three months," she said. "And there are charity hospitals, such as the Leprosy Mission, who will take patients free of charge and eradicate the disease. Sadly, most of my patients are the sole wage earners in their family and cannot afford to be off work for that length of time." As I listened to her, I knew I wanted to be involved in some way.

"What can we do to help?"

"I need to be able to give drug doses daily over three months and to monitor the results on a regular basis," she said.

"What would that cost?"

"For the drugs, in British money, about £8…but we could never persuade someone to stay in hospital that long."

After further discussions we came up with a possible solution and a trial arrangement; one patient, a man in his mid-thirties, pointed the way. He'd been admitted for amputation of his fingers. His wife suffered from encephalitis with blackouts and memory loss, and they had a five-year-old daughter. They lived in a shack and he earned barely enough to feed them so he could not leave them for three months of treatment. This was our plan. The dermatologist would prescribe drugs to take in controlled daily doses and he would visit the hospital once a month to be monitored. The cost of drugs and transport for the whole period, about £30, would be financed by supporters in the UK. The scheme worked and within six months thirty patients were being treated for leprosy. It continued for three years until the doctor left the hospital to be married. Without her the project could not continue.

For a while I arranged, via Jacob, funding for a number of patients at the hospital. One of them was Bindhu who, as well as suffering from lupus and several other conditions, needed a double hip replacement. She was in her early thirties and lived with her mother who had tuberculosis; neither had any way of earning a living. She could not afford to pay for the drugs she needed so we funded her treatment until she died. In the meantime, her mother was trained to use a sewing machine and, despite her health problems, she became skilled enough to support herself.

I have to admit that much of the work in the early days with the elderly and chronically sick was hit and miss. I helped financially when I could raise funds but it was mainly unstructured because for much of the time I was in the hands of others. However, several days spent assisting and visiting on the Dermatology ward during that time taught me a lot about local skin conditions and a great deal about leprosy, knowledge which I was able to put to good use in subsequent projects.

Chapter 10   A Serious Illness: I Near Give Up

My decision to continue staying in the thatched hut in Madurai and experience a little more closely the lives of the people I was helping almost cost me my life. The hut was in an ideal situation, a mile and a half from the city centre of Madurai and within walking distance of the slum, but it was primitive and unhealthy. The water supply and toilet conditions were unsanitary and the only protection against mosquitoes was the net I draped over my bed at night. One evening, midway through the April visit, I returned to the hut exhausted. The day had been a long one with time spent on the streets and at planning meetings with the local charity. I felt hot and feverish but I put this down to dehydration. As I entered the hut I was sick over the floor—presumably another tummy upset, perhaps the result of the coffee made with untreated water I'd carelessly drunk that morning.

I slumped on the bed. My body ached and I was too tired and weak to undress properly. I slept for a while. When I woke I was sweating profusely and my clothes were drenched. I felt sick again and managed to reach the sink. There were cramps in my stomach and the retching became violent and painful. I groped for some bottled water and tried sipping some but I couldn't keep it down. My last memory is a sudden desperate need to get to the toilet before passing out. I came to on the mud floor of the hut. The room was spinning. I was hallucinating in and out of consciousness, seeing creatures crawling on the walls and ceiling. A member of the charity staff, alarmed at my non-appearance, found me. Although I have no clear memory of events I vaguely recall being put into a van and taken to a private hospital. Unfortunately, no one thought to look for the sterile needle pack that I had brought with me and stowed in the cupboard.

It was some time before I realised I was in a hospital bed. I was aware of a cannula in my arm and, looking up, I could see the drip feed coming from a coconut. I learnt later that coconut juice was often used as a substitute for saline in second-rate hospitals. Everything in the room was spinning. Still hallucinating, I was convinced that the bugs on the floor and walls were crawling over my bed covers. I was nauseous and soaking wet from perspiration. I needed to be sick. There was no bell. I called but no one came. I struggled out of bed and, on hands and knees, dragged the drip with me. I reached the toilet only to find it covered in excrement with no way of flushing or cleaning it. I sank to my knees and collapsed. Someone must have found me there and put me back to bed.

The hospital was alive with mosquitoes and, in the absence of a mosquito net, my legs and arms were soon covered with bites. I had no protection against malaria as I'd vomited up my prophylactic pills. I later discovered the needle of the cannula was not sterile and had been used by other patients. In lucid moments, I recognised the symptoms of a severe case of amoebic dysentery. I thought of my comfortable life at home. I thought of Brian and the girls, who didn't even know I was ill. I was alone. I was terrified. I thought I was going to die.

On hearing what had happened, one of the male charity workers, who had worked closely with me on all the projects, rushed to the hospital. It is thanks to his prompt action that I am still alive. The hospital told him that my hallucinations were increasing and if I did not take in more fluids to deal with the dehydration I could be dead within twenty-four hours. He insisted that they move me immediately to another hospital where the conditions and the standard of treatment were considerably better. Gradually over the next few days or so I recovered enough for the hospital to discharge me and I moved back to the hut. I was pitifully weak and that wonderful little housemother, who had looked after me from the very beginning, neglected her duties at the Boys' Home to nurse me back to health and get me back on my feet.

For proper care I needed to return to the UK. The charity booked a train ticket from Madurai to Trivandrum and someone took me to the station. I was helped onto the train as I still found it difficult to stand up. Crammed into a hot compartment, I sat on the hard seat with my head on the wooden headrest. I felt so alone and offered a quick 'Please-God-help-me-to-cope' prayer. My body ached and jarred with the jolting of the train and I just wanted it all to end. Unfortunately, the only train reservation available at such short notice was for a train that stopped for four hours at a small station en route. When I stumbled from the train at the station, the sun was beating down and the temperature was around forty degrees centigrade. The only shade was a small covering near the exit. I staggered towards it alongside the track.

My memories are blurred. All I remember is that I was about to collapse when two strong arms caught me. It was Jacob Joseph from our Boys' Home in Trivandrum, the same Jacob who had stopped me drinking the contaminated orange drink. My prayers had been answered. I was no longer alone. Jacob knew I was ill but no one had told him that I had been discharged from the hospital and was on the train back to Trivandrum. He told me that he had woken up that morning feeling that he had to be with me and had driven to my transit station, arriving in time to find me on the point of collapse. We were both convinced it was a miracle. I still wonder whether I would have survived if he hadn't been there to meet me.

I spent a few days in Trivandrum in my stifling hot room without running water. Jacob and his wife cared for me, and I gradually regained my strength. But about two weeks after the dysentery attack I awoke feeling nauseous again, alternating between shivering and feeling intolerably hot. This was followed by fits so severe that I was literally thrown on to the floor each time. These symptoms continued and, after two days, a local doctor said it was malaria. I moved a short distance across the road to a hotel with air conditioning (£70 a night instead of £2). The fits gradually subsided, but I was incredibly weak, and very frightened. A few days later I managed to get a flight and flew home to the UK where, in the care of my family, I slowly regained my strength.

Over the next few years there were to be other illnesses, including a scare when I stepped on a sickly-looking dog in the slum and got bitten on the ankle. This meant a course of painful injections to back up the pre-exposure rabies vaccinations I had before leaving England. These injections were expensive even in India. I could pay for them, but it made me realise how frightening it must be for the slum dwellers who get bitten and just have to wait and see if they have been infected with the disease.

A serious implication of the shared needle in the first hospital was that I might have contracted HIV. My GP arranged a test that put me through a lot of stress as I waited for the result. Fortunately, the test came back negative. All this left me racked with doubts about the future. Still haunted by the medical problems of my teenage year, I was afraid that a return to India might cause a long-term deterioration in my health. Brian and the girls didn't pressure me but I could see their concern. They didn't want me to go back.

Brian was saying, "Are you sure you want to continue?" and even when those words were not on his lips I knew they were in his mind. The pull of the comfortable life at home with him and the girls was strong and yet I couldn't dismiss from my mind those children in India who needed me. Each night as I lay in bed I was haunted by their faces and I knew that I couldn't let them down. I would have to return at least one more time.

By September, I felt stronger and summoned up the courage to make the trip. Brian got me to Heathrow Airport in good time for my flight but I wouldn't let him wait with me. I wasn't sure how I was going to cope and the thought of him fussing would only add to the stress. I kissed him goodbye and watched him drive away. I was shaking as I entered the terminal and walked hesitantly to the check-in. I handed over my luggage scarcely saying a word. My stomach was churning. I needed to sit somewhere quiet to calm my nerves. All that I had been dreading for the past six months began to crowd in on me. I didn't have to do this. I hated flying at the best of times. I could just walk away and give it all up. I was too weak to look after myself. I had Brian and my girls to care for. Hadn't I done enough?

Yet the boy that I offered a drink to ten years ago in that dusty village still haunted me. A boy who looked into my eyes and for one brief moment knew that someone cared. Behind him, looking over his shoulder, I saw the children who trusted in my promise to return. Satiyan: Raja: Sethuranum: Chandra: Pitchiamani: Pandi and so many more: little expectant faces staring at me, pleading for me to come back. But the horrors of my illness on the last trip replayed in my mind like a recurring nightmare and I became more and more agitated. I stood frozen with fear at the security barrier. I watched the passengers hurrying through but I didn't move.

The command came over the tannoy: "Will remaining passengers for the flight to Colombo (where I was to change planes) please report to the gate immediately. This is the last call." I sat watching the monitor, unable to move, my boarding pass and ticket clenched in my hand. The details on the monitor clicked over, 'Gate closed'. I had missed my flight. I started to cry. A man, noticing my distress, came over and sat next to me. "Are you all right?" I nodded and half smiled through my tears. "I've missed my flight. I'm frightened of flying." How could I explain what was really going on inside me: the terrifying fears that went far beyond flying? He patted my arm in sympathy. "Why don't you go to the desk? I'm sure they'll help."

I sat there a while longer. Suddenly there came into my head some words of Patrick Cornwall, a friend of mine, spoken on the occasion we had last met. "Pat," he said, "I had a dream about you last night. I dreamt that we were all standing on the plain on Judgement Day, and one by one we had to step forward and say who we were. I watched as you stepped forward. You didn't know what to say. Suddenly, a little Indian boy ran forward towards us and cried out, 'This is my Auntie Pat.' 'Yes, I know,' God said, and smiled." The words hit me hard as I sat there. I knew I couldn't leave the street children. But it wasn't going to be easy and I knew I didn't have the strength to do it alone.

It came to me that every experience in my life to date, the army, the holiday camp, family life, nursing, had equipped me for the work ahead. I knew then that I could do it but it was all going to take a little longer. And then I thought of Jacob in Trivandrum, the little group in Madurai and the two doctors. With renewed courage I left my seat, approached the desk and explained what had happened. Miraculously, they found me another flight at no extra cost and a few hours later, I was on my way.

Chapter 11   The Work Expands

I arrived in India, nervous and weak. It was not just the memories of my illness and my traumatic few hours in Heathrow that were pressing on me, but the realisation that if I was to expand the work in the way that I and my growing band of supporters wanted, I would need to unravel my connections with the UK charity I had worked with over the years and establish a totally new charity. I knew this would be difficult not only administratively, because it is not easy setting up charitable trusts in India, but also emotionally because I had been closely involved with people in the UK charity and its counterpart Indian charities for several years. On the other hand, I knew that if the work was to expand in the way that I and my supporters wanted, it had to be done. I realised that this trip would mark a turning point, but I lacked the confidence that I could pull it off.

Soon after my arrival, I walked down onto the beach in Trivandrum and watched the tide wash in and out smoothing the sand. Each time the sea receded the tracks of the fishermen's boats grew fainter and fainter until they disappeared as if they had never existed. Nearby, a crow sat on an old coconut husk, leaning forward and screeching for all its worth—inviting a response. I am by nature a positive and happy person but, on that day, I wondered if what I had achieved so far would be washed away like the boat tracks. I wondered if I would have any more luck than the crow in getting people to listen to me.

I took stock. What points were in my favour? I had talked to hundreds of working children and read widely in the available research material. I had visited projects in Chennai and other cities. I had been accepted into the world of the slum and this acceptance had opened up enormous opportunities to show the people a love many had never known. I had found kindred spirits in some of the excellent project workers who had a real love and commitment to the children. They would be eager to embrace and support me in any new and innovative ventures.

I asked myself what was pushing me on. I had learned that many projects with slum children failed because they had measured success only in terms of a child's health and educational progress. For me these attainments were important, but true success needed to be measured by how a child was responding to love, acceptance and care. I believed this was essential for children who had been beaten, exploited, cheated and treated as vermin. They had no routine, no clear sense of values, no experience of trusting adults, and yet they soaked up love when it was offered. I was sure that giving love would build these children's self-esteem and would eventually lead to deep and lasting change. I then realised that it was for these children I had to carry on. I might feel inadequate but I had to believe that God would help me. I walked back from the beach feeling better and, in the days and visits that followed, with the help of some co-workers, I managed to set in motion the train of events which would eventually lead to the setting up of a new charity, the Vidiyal Trust, in 2006. As the work progressed over the next couple of years, my confidence returned and I felt a renewed peace and contentment as I saw that things were moving in the right direction. As things fell into place, I realised that my earlier visits had prepared me well for the expansion of the work that was underway.

We started a new phase of our work in Madurai. We found a new home to rent and soon had twelve children living there and up to fifty others attending daily and receiving an education. There were another thirty who were regular attendees but who, for different reasons, were not ready for placement and sponsorship. And then there were another fifty or so, mostly rag-pickers and sewage workers, who visited occasionally. We developed various sports programmes and were fortunate to have a professional karate teacher to work with the boys. We opened a Girls' Centre in the Church of South India School nearby and this was soon full to overflowing each evening.

One great concern of the mothers in the slum in Madurai was that their daughters would be pulled into prostitution. We appointed a contact worker with specific responsibility for women's rights and she encouraged the women to share their fears with us. When a mother came to us with concerns for her daughter we would suggest that the girl came onto our sponsorship list, so that her school fees would be paid. One of the mothers told me her eldest daughter had committed suicide for fear of prostitution. She sobbed as she thanked me for arranging schooling for her two other daughters.

Chapter 12   Jacob and the Trivandrum Boys' and Girls' Homes

We began working with our own Trust in Trivandrum. In 1998, I asked Jacob Joseph, my rescuer at the train station, to work with me full time, and we appointed trustees for the new charity. It took us about a year to jump through all the administrative hoops and become accepted as a fully independent organisation. Registering our own Trust proved to be one of our best decisions, as it enabled us later to buy land and put up buildings that would remain our property. UK Charities not registered in India are not able to do this and so ultimately lose control of the land or buildings they purchase. This was not going to happen to us. We soon established our own Boys' and Girls' Homes in Trivandrum in rented buildings. We appointed Jacob-Thomas as caretaker. He was the first boy I had sponsored and at the time homeless and jobless. Jacob Joseph became the director.

My dear friend Jacob Joseph has an interesting background. He was born in 1947, the youngest in a family of three girls and two boys. His grandfather was a presbyter of the Anglican Church of India but none of his four sons wanted to follow in his footsteps. His youngest son Joseph, who was Jacob's father, worked as a civil engineer in Burma for the Burma Mining Corporation. Although not a priest, he was in charge of a church designated for the labourers and took the services when a priest was not available. Jacob's mother worked alongside him in this ministry, organizing the wives of the managers to work with the local widows and orphans, irrespective of their caste, colour or creed. Tragically, his father died when Jacob was five and his mother had quite a struggle to raise her family alone.

Jacob's mother wanted him to enter the priesthood but he'd set his heart on joining the army. However, ill health sabotaged that dream and he became a teacher. As Jacob told me this, I smiled thinking how much his story was like my own. After qualifying as a teacher, Jacob took a post overseas in Ethiopia and married Jesse, who was the youngest daughter of a minister of the Church of South India. "It was an arranged marriage," he told me, "but the instant I saw her I fell in love." In 1974, he moved to Nigeria where he worked for twelve years at the Government Commercial College in Zaria, serving as Vice Principal for the last three. On returning to India in the late 1980s he felt a calling to social work and was appointed as head of the boys' home in Trivandrum that had been the focus of my very first trip.

I enjoyed meeting Jacob and Jesse on each visit. I was thrilled at how Jacob's thinking dovetailed into mine. He had sacrificed status and wealth to work with the poor of India, without praise or recognition, and the more time I spent with him, the more I admired him. Our working relationship and strong friendship has now lasted sixteen years, and he has been the life-force of our work in Kerala State.

Chapter 13   Trips Away

I believed that the children who had lived every day of their lives in the slum could benefit enormously from a trip away. Remembering the magic of my own childhood holidays, I suggested taking the twenty-five boys from our Trivandrum home on a day trip to the sea side. The boys had never travelled by train before and were wildly excited. Jacob and I arrived with them at the station early in the morning. The train was on the opposite platform and in the absence of a bridge, we had to drop down about five feet onto the tracks and shepherd the lively boys safely to the other side. Not a task for those of a nervous disposition.

The train took us around one side of the Western Ghats, an extensive range of mountains, a marvel to the boys who had never seen mountains before. At Nagacoil we transferred to a public bus for the final eight miles. The bus, like most busses in India, was a single-decker that had seen better days. There was no closable door and the only air conditioning came from the doorway and the windows (open gaps with a few rusty bars). The bus was overcrowded but somehow we fought our way through the mass of bodies and grabbed some spaces. We were so cramped it was hard to breathe. The journey was only half an hour but, in the intense heat, it seemed an eternity.

The first stop of the day was the Ghandi Memorial where we had to remove our shoes. I found it difficult to walk on the blistering hot concrete in bare feet but the boys had no problem. Then it was ice creams all round and later a lunch of *masal dosai* (paper-thin pancakes). After lunch, we took the ferry to a rocky island just offshore. The boys thought the trip was fantastic but all I can remember is the vast number of people who needed to do something to our tickets and the far from seaworthy ferry boat belching out noxious diesel fumes. We returned to Trivandrum by bus—a five hour journey with a driver who used his horn more than the gears. How I wished I'd had the presence of mind to take earplugs! What made the trip worthwhile was the joy and excitement of the boys. It was a day I will never forget.

This reminds me of another traumatic bus journey. On that occasion I was travelling alone and had become quite concerned when, long before our scheduled arrival time, the bus driver pulled into a village square and told all the passengers to get off. We did but then, to my horror, he drove away. As I watched the bus disappear, several people in the square started calling: "Madamma, Madamma," which means white woman. I was obviously a novelty—the first Madamma most of the people had seen. Soon I was surrounded; I was poked, my hair was examined and my cheeks pinched–the Indian kiss! I was really scared. All of my luggage was on the bus, and these were the days before mobile phones. I headed for a Coca Cola sign, which strangely seemed to represent a modicum of security. I was still surrounded by people speaking and shouting but I felt terribly alone. I didn't know where I was and could no longer see any of my travelling companions. I wondered how I was going to be rescued. To my great relief, the bus eventually returned. The explanation was simple: one of the tyres had a puncture and the driver had taken it to be repaired. In hindsight, I thought that the feelings of fear and confusion I had experienced might be similar to the feelings of people suffering from Alzheimer's.

The experience of that day lay dormant in my mind until two years later when one of the co-workers and I were reviewing the Madurai drop-in centre project. "You know Pat," he said, "what these children need is a break from the slums: somewhere new and exciting." "You mean like a day out," I said as memories of the trip two years earlier came flooding back. "Yes, in a way. But I was really thinking of more like four days…a camp." I thought back to that holiday camp in Gorleston all those years ago, when I spent my days providing entertainment for a bunch of lively children. I had the experience. I was prepared. The idea was brilliant and we started to make plans there and then. We would take a hundred slum children from the Madurai drop-in centre to Veli, a seaside resort just outside Trivandrum.

The original hundred were whittled down to seventy-one boys and four girls as a number of parents were suspicious of our motives, believing that the camp was a ruse to steal the children's kidneys. I booked a large youth hostel to house the children and arranged the catering with an Indian coffee shop, ensuring that the children had lots of protein and fruit which was not normally part of their diet. Weeks later, Jacob and I were standing on the platform at Trivandrum station, waiting for the Madurai train. Seventy-five children leapt off, screaming with delight as they swarmed around us. It must have looked as though we were under attack as several policeman hurried to investigate.

When we arrived at the Youth Hostel, the space and the comfort staggered the children. For the first time in their lives they would sleep alone in their own bed. For the first time in their lives they would be able to shower—and not only once but three times a day. The first breakfast was bedlam. I had arranged generous portions of food—*iddli* (steamed rice cakes), *samber* (a very spicy gravy), vegetable *dahl* (a lentil and vegetable mix), and a cup of milk for each child, collected by our driver each morning. How ignorant I was. It had never occurred to me that the children would assume that the breakfast spread before them was their only meal of the day. The moment they caught their first glimpse of the food, they stampeded into the dining room, almost knocking me over—seventy-five children, fighting for food to squirrel away for later. When order was restored I explained to them that they were going to be fed three times a day but, this was so hard to believe that it took a couple of days before I could get them queuing in an orderly fashion.

After breakfast, we went down to the beach and they saw the sea for the first time. The sheer wonder on their faces reduced me to tears. TS, a nine-year-old boy with severe cerebral palsy, whom we had found abandoned in a sewer, could hardly believe his eyes. The look of wonder throughout the long train journey became a beautiful smile as we drove through lush forests of coconut trees. And then, as we lifted him onto the sea wall, this young silent boy lifted his arm and spoke his first word—"Look". I hope that memories of that wonderful day helped ease some of the pain of his terrible childhood. Now a grown man, just hearing the word 'sea' evokes that same look of wonder. The children were overawed and a little nervous to begin with but it wasn't long before they were diving into the waves and splashing each other in joyful play. Other activities at the camp included sing songs, beach games, flower making, talent shows, shell collecting and the camp Olympics. The children's laughter and happy chatter filled the days from early morning until late at night. There was so much to teach them but as I watched them being children I was deliriously happy.

Using the toilets was another new experience to children who normally used a space behind their slum hut. Within a day the cubicles were filthy and the smell unbearable. I obtained a quantity of disinfectant and taught the children how to keep them clean. I taught lessons on personal hygiene and gave each child some soap and a comb. We used every opportunity to get the children to talk about, sing about, and act out the problems of being a street child. Many had wounds on their hands and feet from rag picking. I made a special visit to Trivandrum to buy gauze, antiseptic, plasters and other first aid equipment to treat them. I spent hours picking maggots out of wounds and then cleaning them.

The children had scarcely enough clothing to cover their bodies and none of them had shoes. Thanks to a collection in Norfolk from the villages of Brundall, Blofield, and Postwick, we were able to give 'new' clothes to each child. Such was the novelty of these that one little girl was seen showing a friend her four pairs of new pants – she was wearing all of them at the same time. On the third day, we took the children to the zoo where they saw lions, tigers, giraffes, elephants and other wild animals they had not only never seen but some they had never even heard of.

An enduring memory for me is the last night of that first camp. In the twilight the children stood in a circle, each holding a lighted candle. They stood quietly for a while and then began to sing 'We shall overcome'. As I looked from face to face, each brightly shining in the flickering light, I stepped back into the shadows, trembling and tearful.

When we returned the children to Madurai, the reception from the slum families was all that we could have wished. They could see the difference in their children and we had established a trust between us that would grow and deepen in the years to come. "The camp is one of the best things we've done," said one of the project workers afterwards and I agreed. We decided to make the camps a regular feature of the Street Children Project but wisdom dictated that we would have two camps a year with smaller numbers of children. Over the years, they have been a great success. The children are loving, exuberant, and noisy, and afterwards they are noticeably cleaner and better behaved.

Chapter 14   Train Journeys and Meeting Mother Teresa

I have spent many hours travelling on trains from one part of India to another, often in the company of boisterous, excited children on the way to one of our camps. It is the safest and best way to cover long journeys. In my early days the stations and trains, all of them diesels liveried in dark chocolate brown, were not noted for their luxury. The trains were home to large numbers of rats, a particular problem to passengers travelling through the night. Sometimes a street child would board a train, hoping to earn a few rupees by sweeping up the mouse and rat droppings. There was no air-conditioning and the toilets were filthy. Travelling second class meant plastic covered seats that converted at night into bunks. A narrow corridor ran down the centre of the train. On one side were compartments with two three-tiered bunks and, on the other side, two-tiered bunks divided from the corridor by only a curtain. The smell of bodies was overpowering and the noise unabating. Over the years, there have been considerable improvements and although cockroaches and mosquitoes still travel by train, the rats are mostly confined to the track. The toilets smell as bad as ever. For a while I paid a small supplement and travelled First Class, but I soon realised it was safer to travel in Second Class where the sheer numbers of passengers gave added security. What eventually convinced me was the occasion when, alone in my bunk in a First Class single compartment, I woke in the dead of night to someone banging on the door. "Pat, Pat, Pat, open the door quickly!" I climbed down from the bunk and was about to open the door when it occurred to me that no one on the train knew my name. Then it dawned on me that my name was on a label outside the compartment. Wisely, I kept the door shut and the caller went away. Later, I learnt this was a well-known trick used by robbers to gain access.

Refreshments are available both on the trains and at the stations. Even in the middle of the night, the air echoes with cries of "Chai, chai, chai, coffee, coffee, coffee." Chai is an Indian tea spiced with cinnamon and made with boiled milk and is often accompanied by sweetmeats and pastries. Train journeys, while much safer than travelling by road, are not without their hazards. To cross from one platform to another to change trains, passengers jump down a couple of feet onto the tracks and then, keeping a sharp lookout, may have to cross as many as four sets of tracks to reach the other side.

A journey I make on every visit is the one between Trivandrum and Madurai. It takes about nine hours and involves travelling down to the southern tip of India before looping back up again to Madurai. The train passes through vast built up urban areas, lush green paddy fields, leafy coconut groves, the Windy Valley with its seven hundred wind turbines, dry desert scrub and the towering mountains of the Western Ghats. On the last four hours of the journey the train crosses the plains. Drought is now a serious problem in large parts of India and over the nineteen years I have been making this journey, I have seen dramatic changes in the scenery. Where rivers once rushed by in full flood, now there are only cracked, dry riverbeds. As there is no longer the water to grow crops, hundreds of people have migrated to the edges of the city and have set up makeshift homes on the large riverbed leading into Madurai. However, what I remember most about these journeys are the people I have met.

At each of the village halts along the route, the cry went up, "Madamma!" and there was a rush of children to see this oddity passing by. One of the refreshment wallahs, with his tray of sweetmeats, came to know me and always rushed up to me calling: "Previously, previously". He did this so often that I forever referred to him by that name. On one journey, I fell into conversation with a family from Kolcata (Calcutta) who had travelled to Southern India for a wedding. The man was a Doctor and he had two well-dressed children. "Why do you bother with us?" he asked on hearing about my work. "Because I love India," I replied. It seemed an inadequate way to describe a work that on the one hand gives me so much peace and happiness and on the other so much pain and frustration because I can do so little. When the journey ended he gave me 200 rupees (then about £4) towards the work.

An old friend of mine Provost Richard Howard spent his early years in India. Just before he died aged 97, he asked himself, "Why has God put me here?" It is a question that I have asked myself and it was on that same journey that I received my answer. It started when I got off the train at the wrong station, thinking that I'd arrived at Sengottai. Just as the train was starting to move off, I realised my mistake. I leapt into the nearest carriage and, a little frightened by the experience, I sat on the floor by the door to get my breath back. Seated on the dirty floor next to me was a lady with a large basket half full of spiral wheat cakes she had been selling on the train. She looked about seventy but was probably no more than fifty. Her face was badly lined, she was painfully thin and desperately poor, but she hadn't given up. We shared the same space in silence for about twenty minutes. She glanced at me a few times. I tried to put my hand out in friendship but she was having none of that. As she left the train at the next stop I gave her 100 rupees (about £2), probably more than she earned in a week. She took it without a word or smile. As I watched her limp down the platform without a backward glance, I knew that she and others like her were the reason I was there.

Of all my train journeys, the most memorable was my six day round trip from Trivandrum to Kolcata to meet Mother Teresa. The visit was important to me because her concept of unconditional love was an inspiration for my work in India, and I wanted to see if I could learn anything more. It was February 5th, 1997 and Mother Teresa was dying. Jacob and I set off on a journey that would take at least three days each way. The train on the first leg of the journey to Cochin was clean, reasonably comfortable and air-conditioned. I checked the toilets, always a concern of mine, and found they were passable.

We had a two hour wait at Cochin which meant sitting on the platform as there were no waiting rooms. The train we took on the second leg of our journey to Kolcata (about forty hours) was not so clean. At the start of the journey, a small rat, apparently eager to leave, startled Jacob as it scurried across his arm, over the seat, and out the door. The air-conditioning was not working. We shared a four-berth sleeper with a young middle class couple. The woman had a shrill voice and talked on and off all night which, coupled with the noise of the train, made it a long wearisome journey.

The mile after mile of slums around Chennai were distressing to see but, as the train progressed, the scenery improved as we passed through tobacco and mango plantations. Leaving the plantations behind, the terrain opened up into a vast emptiness of flat arid land with no sign of people: another reminder of the increasing shortage of water in India. Finally, we reached Kolkata, a teeming metropolis of some four million people.

There was a notable difference in the temperature. We had left Trivandrum in thirty-eight degrees and it was now sixteen. Kolkata is a very modern city, rich in its British heritage, with parks, sports stadia, multi-storey buildings and even a clone of St Paul's Cathedral. On that first evening, I went to a fete in the grounds of the cathedral and I could easily have been at an English Church Garden Party.

The following day Jacob and I went on a prearranged visit to the Motherhouse, the building where Mother Teresa started her work, now much bigger, and the headquarters of the Missionaries of Charity. Sister Doris, one of the most senior staff, met us and explained that Mother Teresa was drifting in and out of consciousness and not up to seeing visitors. "I understand how important this visit is to you," she said. "I've made an appointment for you to see her tomorrow if she is well enough."

During our waiting time we visited the Kalighat home for the terminally ill. It was not so much a ward as a massive hall, almost a warehouse, with a raised platform down one wall. There were about sixty people on pallets and camp beds. It was overcrowded with bed after bed of indescribable suffering, people whose manner of dying reflected the suffering life they had lived. Their arms were so thin that I feared they would break as they hugged me. Most had advanced tuberculosis and I could hear the rasping noise of uninterrupted coughing long before I entered the hall. The patients lay there dying with blood on their faces and clothes and on the floor; their bodies were convulsed in pain with each gasp for breath as their lungs slowly filled. And yet, there was an overwhelming atmosphere of peace and love, which came from the Sisters who epitomised all that Mother Teresa stood for. Eventually you learn to become hardened to suffering, which is just as well, for if not you would spend your time in tears and be powerless to help.

The other place I visited was Prem Dam, the home for the destitute. This was an even larger warehouse on the edge of a slum. It had previously been used for storing paint. Beds for about two hundred and fifty people were crammed so close it was very difficult to walk between them. Medical treatment was limited to rehydrating the patients, who were fed and loved until they were fit enough to return to their wretched lives on the streets. Mother Teresa's view was that her job was to relieve their suffering and it was the Government's job to solve the overall social and medical problems. All we could do was to go from bed to bed hugging, stroking and being part of something I find hard to put into words. There was a beautiful atmosphere of love and peace and the smiles I was given reduced me to tears.

The next morning Jacob and I returned to the Motherhouse, greeted this time by Sister Hyacinth. "Mother is very weak, but wait and see," she advised. We went into the courtyard to wait and I took a couple of photographs. Sister Hyacinth reappeared. "Come," she said and took me by the hand.

We climbed a flight of stone stairs leading to Mother Teresa's bedroom, a tiny room measuring about eight feet by five feet with a spotlessly clean stone floor. Mother Teresa was lying on a narrow bed along one wall. There was a mirror on the opposite wall and beneath it a bucket and a bowl. There was so little space, that I had to walk in sideways. Mother Teresa, weak as she was, struggled to a sitting position and patted the bed for me to join her. She pulled back her veil. Nervously I took her hands and she pulled me to her and hugged me. "Thank you for letting me come," I said softly. She smiled and replied, "Don't stop. Don't stop loving." My meeting was over in minutes. Jacob went in as I left.

I was overwhelmed and felt so weak that I had a job to get down the stairs. Most of all I was inspired and no longer felt inadequate. I am not comparing myself with Mother Teresa but I saw that, although our projects were different from hers, they were just as important. I was so fortunate to see her as she had not seen an outsider for several months. A few months later she died.

Jacob and I sat down for a minute or two before leaving the house. I was still recovering from my serious illness but, as we sat there, I knew that my work would continue whatever the obstacles. Mother Teresa inspired me that day and has continued to inspire me ever since.

Chapter 15   Exploited Hotel Workers

The broken sign hung lopsidedly above the door. The faded letters said 'Hotel' but that was an exaggeration. It was nothing more than a cheap eating-house near the market. Its white façade of peeling paint was not out of place among the other hotels spaced at intervals along a street of cheap shops and market stalls. I walked through the open door and saw people jostling with one another for a spot to eat. Dirt, paper and spilt food swarming with flies lay on the floor. Upstairs the seating was for a higher class of clientele, who sat on plain wooden benches to eat at tables of cheap wood, covered with chipped plastic veneer. The cracks were ingrained with stale food. The walls were so discoloured with grease and dirt that it was difficult to determine the original décor.

I watched the boy serving the tables. He was obviously malnourished and looked much younger than the legal age limit of fifteen years but I knew no one bothered to enforce the law. His uniform was a stained maroon tunic top and torn shorts. He wore nothing on his feet. It was late morning and he looked tired. He had probably worked non-stop since six am and, apart from a short break, he would work on until six pm. Tomorrow, his shift might be noon to midnight. He would work a seven-day week with no holidays or days off. When he finished work, he might be allowed to take a bucket of leftover slops to sell in the streets and in the slums and hopefully make a few rupees. Then he would either sleep under the tables in the eating-house or, if he was lucky, in a room at the back where he would share a bed with other boys.

The boy cleared the tables as fast as he could, watched by his boss, an obese man in a sweat stained t-shirt. Tucked into his belt was a cloth, smelling of rotten vegetables and ingrained with bits of stale food. Occasionally, the boss would pull out the cloth, wipe down an empty table with it, and then rinse it in a rusty bucket of grey water.

The boy kept staring at me. I guess he thought it strange to see a lone white woman sitting at a table. Women did not usually frequent eating-houses but then the English were a strange people. The owner approached my table and handed me a greasy, barely legible, plastic covered menu. I ordered thin potato pancakes and a cup of tea. Having taken my order he turned from the table, gripped the boy by his arm and propelled him towards the kitchen. After a short while they returned with my food. The owner placed the plate of pancakes on the table and supplemented them with a dollop of spicy sauce ladled from a bucket held by the boy. It was not appetizing but I needed to eat something. The owner then placed a stainless steel bowl containing a glass cup on the table. I indicated that the cup and bowl were dirty with bits of dried food around the brim. He scowled, smoothed his sweaty hands down his apron, picked up the cup, spat on his fingers and wiped them around the rim. He then proceeded to fill it with boiled tea and milk from a large beaker. Throughout, the boy stood in the background waiting to jump the moment his boss barked an instruction.

He watched me slyly as I ate the pancakes and drank the tea. I caught his eye and smiled at him. He turned his back but after a few minutes he could not resist peeking again to see if I was still looking. I smiled again. This time he smiled back. When I left, I handed him a five rupee note and then, out of sight of the owner, I slipped a fifty rupee note into his pocket. I winked and smiled. He was the first of many hotel boys I came to know.

One was Pandi. Before working in the hotel he had led a pleasanter life. He had reached the seventh standard at school and was able to read and write. But his parents, who were coolies, ran up a debt of about £100 for medical fees, which they could not repay on their meagre earnings. So Pandi, to earn money to help repay the debt, was taken out of school and bonded to a hotel for a year. His life had become one of relentless drudgery devoid of love and care.

Another was Mariapann. He was eleven, but he could have been mistaken for a six-year-old. His mother had died when he was about four. His father had remarried but, two years later, had died himself. The boy's stepmother had no affection for him, so she bonded him to a hotel and, each month, collected his wages--150 rupees (about £2.80). When I first met him he had been working as a hotel boy for two years. He did not like to be touched and shied away from all physical contact.

Then there was the boy who, on the death of his parents when he was twelve, had been bonded to support his two younger sisters. And the boy who worked fourteen hours a day for 5 rupees and his food. And the boy…and the boy…there were so many of them, bonded in so many hotels, with no one to love or care for them. The more I learnt about the conditions of hotel workers, the more I became concerned for their welfare. They did not fall into the same category as street children because they were employed throughout the day and had less freedom to roam the streets. But their lives were lives of drudgery, frequent brutality and sometimes sexual abuse. In Trivandrum, it was estimated that there were six hundred boys, mostly from the neighbouring state of Tamil Nadu. In Madurai, the figure was a shocking six thousand.

The word 'hotel' is a misnomer as they are, in reality, cheap roadside cafes with the children who work in them bonded to the owners for a specific period. The law in India says that no child under fifteen can be employed, so any working boy, when asked his age, will always say, "Fifteen". But while it is easy to condemn child labour, clamping down on the practice would condemn many families to starvation. Most of the children are there either to earn money to pay off a family debt, to pay for expensive medical treatment, or perhaps to supplement the family income when the parents are sick and unable to work. In some cases their earnings are used to save a younger sister from prostitution, by keeping her in school. Sometimes, by the time a boy leaves a hotel at the conclusion of his bonded period, his family has died or moved away.

Although the hotel workers are overworked, sad, lonely children, the upside is that they eat regularly and have a place to live. They know that if they were not in the hotels they would be rag-picking, working in the sewers, or worse. I wanted to do something for these boys, but at that time I was preoccupied with dealing with the creation of our own boys' home in Trivandrum and bedding down the street children project in Madurai. But it was putting together the street children project that first sparked the glimmer of an idea. I had spent a lot of my spare time in Trivandrum visiting eating houses, usually in the morning when I was able to indulge my love of the crispy fried breakfast breads called *puris*! This was so that I could see some of the boys working there. Jacob shared my concern for these boys and set up a meeting with a member of the Hotel Workers Association in Trivandrum.

The Association is a voluntary body whose objective is to ensure that all members work to a common code of conduct. I met with Kannon, the Association Secretary in Trivandrum, who himself managed a large eating-house. Beginning to feel at ease with him, I was bold enough one day to raise the subject of the welfare of the boys. "Surely, you can't be happy with the condition the boys work in?" I said. "No…," he answered cautiously, probably wondering where this was leading. "I've been worried about the boys for some time but I'm not sure what our Association can do to improve conditions that will be accepted by our members?" "Why don't you have some form of monitoring system looking at the boys' welfare?" I suggested. "And…" I was getting excited now, "…allow the boys recreational time during the day. Maybe even go so far as to have annual camps for the boys to give them a break from the hard life they lead?" Kannon was surprisingly receptive.

"I like the idea. Can you help us in this, Pat? I will see to it the Association gives you every support." Me and my big mouth! But it was something I knew we could do and it would improve the boys' lives. As the Association only existed in Trivandrum I consulted with Jacob and we decided to initiate a small pilot scheme there. With Kannon's help we selected eight hotels. Our idea was to provide a base where the boys would come during their break period to play games, watch TV, do some gardening and where, in a loving and caring environment, they could just be children.

First we had to find suitable premises--a place with washing facilities that was big enough for them to relax and play. The Hotel Owners Association put us in contact with a bank manager who was vacating his house for two years. After a lot of persuasion, he eventually agreed to let his house for the use of the boys. It was expensive but it had a third of an acre of land, wildly overgrown, but full of coconut trees. The bank manager stored his property in the upper floor and we used the ground floor. The house had been empty for some time and was filthy and full of cockroaches but, after a clean and a coat of paint, it was ideal for our purpose. When everything was ready, there was an inauguration ceremony, almost compulsory in India. Several hotel owners, the committee of the Hotel Owners Association, a doctor, a priest and eleven boys attended. What saddened me was that the adults sat away from the boys and would not associate with them. Jacob became the overseer of the project and Rajan, a taxi driver, became the project worker/driver, collecting the boys by car and returning them at the end of the session. The estimated cost of the project was about £30 per boy per year.

The boys worked from six am to ten pm each day with two two-hour rest periods, one in the morning and one in the late afternoon. They loved the car ride from their hotel to the centre but we soon discovered they had no concept of play; all they had ever done was sleep and work. Gradually, they grew accustomed to relaxing. *Carroms* was the most popular game. Similar to snooker, it is played on a board the size of a coffee table and involves flicking discs into pockets. We also introduced magazines and television. In time, the boys asked for basketball, badminton and football, which they played enthusiastically when we could prise them away from the television. There were some teething problems. One hotel did not send boys because they were convinced we were trying to convert them to Christianity, but gradually barriers were broken down and the hotel owners themselves began to appreciate the benefits. The boys were healthier, happier and worked more willingly. As the project expanded, many hotel owners realised that the boys had the right to a life outside the hotel and some of the owners of the better hotels began to give their boys a day off each week.

After six months we moved to a new house that had a better layout and was cheaper. What was wonderful was that, as the work developed, the Hotel Workers Association became more and more supportive. As one owner said, "You have made us look at the boys differently." By the year 2000 the work was so effective that, following an exposé in the paper, there was a tightening of the law in Trivandrum concerning the employment of underage boys generally. This, coupled with a more responsible approach by the hotel owners themselves, meant that the project in Trivandrum was no longer necessary.

Unfortunately, this was not the case in Madurai where there was no Hotel Owners Association to enforce the legislation. However, I was keen for the model we had in Trivandrum to be copied and so, once we had found suitable premises, we set up a centre for the Madurai hotel boys. Under the supervision of our street children project the best we could do was to give the boys a chance to play, provide a basic medical programme for them, and introduce tuition and skill training. In that when they left the hotels they could feed into our workshop network.

The project meant that sixty to a hundred hotel boys in Madurai had the opportunity to be children for a few hours a week. Muthukumar, the excellent social worker who built up this project still works with us today. He was to become as important a friend and co-worker as Jacob, and he now directs all of our Trust's work in Madurai.

Chapter 16   A Child of the Gutter

During my visit to Madurai in September 1999, I found a young boy dying
on the ground in a back alley behind our Centre. He was face down in the
gutter among the sewage waste and almost unconscious. He was lying
naked under the merciless sun and covered in excrement. Judging by the
size of his feet, he was probably twelve years old but he looked about
seven. He'd been raped. He'd been beaten. His bones pushed against his
paper-thin skin, striving to break through. His mouth was edged with
infected sores and dried specks of blood from tuberculosis. He had
chronic dysentery and AIDS. If we hadn't found him, he would have been
collected with the other garbage, for that was all he was to many of the
people who passed him by in the street.

I asked for water to be brought and one of our boys washed him. Then I
sat him on my lap, and tried to feed him. The only way to do this was to
put small amounts directly into his mouth. Clean clothes were brought for
him. He soiled again but watching one of our older boys wash him with
such tenderness brought tears to my eyes. The boy had been abandoned.
He couldn't speak due to the injuries he had suffered and there was
nothing on him to identity him or his family. We called him Joseph. I
picked him up again and he snuggled into me like a baby, his little bony
frame nestling in search of comfort and love. He didn't mind me touching
him and from the day we found him, he wouldn't let me put him down.

For six days I nursed him. I hugged him; I kissed him; I cuddled him. It
was perhaps the first time in his brief life that someone had shown love to
him and he wasn't letting go. When it came time for me to return to the
UK, my attachment to him had grown so strong that I found it difficult to
leave. "What are we going to do with him?" I asked the senior worker.
"He's too sick for us to care for him. We don't have the facilities or the
staff. You have to accept that he's dying, Pat. I think the best we can do is
to find a hospital to look after him in his last few days." Much as I wanted
I could stay no longer. I'd been away six weeks and had a new job waiting

for me back home. It broke my heart to leave him and I made my colleague promise to find him somewhere comfortable. One of the workers found him a place in a mission hospital. He was not happy to leave him there, lying on a mat alongside dozens of other similar children, but it was the best he could find. Joseph died three weeks later.

I have seen many children dying on the streets because of illness or disabilities. On one occasion I found a small boy lying in sewage, with the hogs rooting around him. His limbs were badly misshapen, probably from rickets. He had rolled there from a nearby hut. He had been left alone by his parents while they went rag-picking, trying to earn money for food.

There have been many like Joseph before and since, but for some reason I cannot explain Joseph affected me the deepest of all. Joseph was the catalyst that made me decide never again to take a sick child to another organisation. I could not bear the thought of another child coming into our care and being passed to another institution to die. I discussed these issues with the other workers in the centre knowing that it wasn't just a matter of providing accommodation. These children needed varying degrees of specialist care and education. Everyone agreed and, from our discussions, the idea of a place for the care of disabled street children was born—a place where they would be nurtured and encouraged to lead as normal a life as possible. I asked for it to be called Joseph's House. It could have no other name.

I received some generous donations from the UK that allowed us to find three-storey premises in Madurai away from the city centre. We painted it bright colours, decorated it with cartoon characters from Walt Disney, and furnished it with lots of toys I brought from the UK. I wanted it to be cheerful—a place of joy. I thought finding the right staff would be difficult but we were able to obtain the services of a wonderful cook, a housemother and the part-time services of a doctor.

When I visited India six months later the project was two months underway. Our first child was Tamil, a young boy, who had been found in the Mellawassal slum. At first I thought he was about eighteen months old. In fact, he was four and a half. His teenage mother had been a rag-picker. He suffered from cerebral palsy and had no control over his limbs, but he radiated a delightful smile. When he arrived, he could not speak and was incontinent but, after a year, although still only weighing twelve pounds, he was strong enough to be de-wormed. He disgorged eighteen worms. It was difficult to get him to respond to stimuli, until at one of the camps, I took him down to the sea for his first view of the waves. The effect was electrifying as slowly he lifted up his arms and pointed excitedly at the water. From that ground breaking moment, he gradually improved. He gained weight and started to control his limbs better and make noises. He began to walk between parallel bars and continued to progress, warming everyone with his lovely smile.

Iyyapan joined us when he was eight. He had a withered leg and crawled around on his hands and feet. He progressed so much that eventually he was well enough to attend a special school and return to his family each evening. Yasmin was brought to us by the police who found her on the streets, incapable of fending for herself. When she arrived, she just sat in the corner with a doll, rocking herself, hunched up in front of a mirror. It was difficult to treat her until we traced her history. She'd been placed in an asylum, we think at the age of three, because she was mentally disabled. The asylum had caught fire and many patients died shackled to their beds. Yasmin was one of eight rescued and taken to hospital having inhaled a lot of smoke. When she was better, the hospital put her out on the streets, because no one had come to claim her. We arranged a year of physiotherapy to enable her to stand up and gradually she responded to the love around her.

We started with three or four residential children with another three attending on a daily basis. Gradually numbers increased. In many ways, it was more of a hospice than a home as most of the children had a short life expectancy. It was difficult to deal with some of the special needs children and a moment's inattention could bring disaster. On one occasion, a boy sneaked into the kitchen area and took some matches. The first sign that there was anything wrong was smoke coming from the bedroom where he'd started a fire. This was a matter of serious concern, especially as there have been several disastrous fires in institutional homes in India. Despite the difficulties and problems of dealing with these children, Joseph's House was a special place with a great wave of love washing through it. The excellent housemother is working with me today in our home for the elderly.

As our work grew on different sites in Madurai, the various projects were proving difficult to manage. The need to restructure our accommodation brought another significant change to the work.

Chapter 17   A New Children's Centre in Madurai

As the success of the drop-in centre in Madurai progressed, with one hundred and forty plus children swarming around us each evening, it soon became apparent that our resident children (mostly orphans) and the children in Joseph's House needed a space of their own. Struggling to speak above the noise of kids screaming with joy as they played, I said to the others: "We can't go on like this. We're bursting at the seams and it's not fair to the residential children who must feel as though their home is being invaded." They nodded in agreement. We needed to rent a larger place, but not only would this cost more it would be difficult to find a place with the right number of rooms. Later that evening over a meal the subject came up again. "What if we buy some land and build a place of our own?" I suggested. "We could build all the rooms we wanted plus a play area outside and amalgamate the Trust Home and Joseph's House."

My enthusiasm for the idea was taking me ahead of the others but I could see they were receptive. I took a serviette and together we sketched out the layout of our dream building. As we began our planning, we found out that the authorities would not allow us to put up the building we wanted in the city itself. The home would have to be built at least two miles from the slum. The disadvantage of this would be the need for transport. The advantage was that, as land outside the city was cheaper, we would be able to afford a bigger building with more playing space for the children.

We wanted the new centre to be a solid building, made of brick and concrete and we thought we could build it for about £26,000. Half the money we needed was available. When I returned to the UK and told people of our plans the response was enthusiastic. We found people wanting to sponsor rooms in the building and contributions flooded in. Within six months we had enough funds to go ahead. We purchased some land and sat down to design the ideal place that would be more of a home than an institution. We built into it the capacity to expand. It would be a single storey building but with a high parapet surrounding the large flat roof which would give us a lot more usable space. There would be a hall fifty feet by twenty feet, dormitories, dining hall, medical room, kitchen and toilets. There would also be a room for the special needs children plus a bedroom for a staff member. Overall, the building would have 50,000 square feet of space. Importantly the foundations would be made strong enough to take an additional storey later if the need arose.

Amazingly, the house was completed in early 2002. The excitement as thirty-two resident and sixteen handicapped children moved in was explosive. The children rushed from room to room trying all the doors, flushing the toilets and admiring their own cupboard and bed mat. You'd have thought we'd given them the Taj Mahal to live in. Unfortunately, the interior with its whitewashed walls didn't have a homely feel to it, but then a Norfolk Charity called HOPE (Helping Other People Everywhere) came to our aid. This charity is supported by experienced tradesmen in the building trade, who raise their own funds and give their time and expertise to renovate medical centres and other buildings in different parts of the world. After a delay, due to a threatened military conflict between India and Pakistan, the HOPE team arrived in January 2003 to put the decorative finish to the building.

We had a hectic but hilarious time buying the paint and all the equipment but, when the team had done their work, the transformation was amazing. An added bonus was that the team members taught several boys the skills of decorating and two of the older boys now earn money by offering their decorating service to others. We finished up with a brightly coloured building, blue in the entrance hall and buttercup yellow in the main meeting hall. Built-in cupboards were constructed in the dormitories and the children were allowed to select their colour of choice for their locker. A small room, painted in the yellow and green colours of Norwich City Football Club, was reserved for me. In memory of a relative who had died in a road accident, an Indian family donated an adjoining plot of land. The HOPE team in seven days not only transformed the building but also helped to level several tons of topsoil, put in timber edging, and plant a wonderful garden for the children.

Once the building was operational, we took another step in August 2003 when, to my delight, we received accreditation to start a Nursery School for three- to six-year olds. This all happened about the time when some eighty families, who lived in shacks on the edge of the slum alongside the railway track were made homeless. Without warning the railway company had sent in bulldozers and razed the shacks to the ground. The families were there illegally and, as they were untouchables, they had no rights. Some families found space in another part of the slum but others were forced to live on the pavements. Without our help, the children of these families would have been left alone all day as their parents tried to rebuild their lives and earn a living; they would have had no hope of an education.

Our original intention was to run the school on the roof of the new building but this proved impractical as, despite the high parapet, the teachers were terrified a child might fall over. So, we made a few changes. The Joseph's House children had free reign of the hall during the day, but, as most of them had limited mobility, they didn't really need that amount of space. So we relocated them to a couple of smaller rooms with convenient access to the garden, and the large hall became our school building. We employed a Montessori-trained teacher assisted by one of our street girls, who had done some teacher training. The Montessori Method of teaching, based on the belief that each child should be valued as an individual, was compatible with our own philosophy. By 2005 there were sixty children in the school, wearing uniforms made by our tailoring unit. The boys wore shorts and check shirts and the girls check shifts.

We transported the children from the slum to the school each day by auto-rickshaw and a bus provided by a Rotary Club in the UK. They were greeted with a milky drink when they arrived, served a cooked lunch in the middle of the day, and given tea and biscuits before they went home. We also arranged regular medical check-ups. Before long, we had a long waiting list of children wanting to attend. We began to consider the need for additional classrooms and increasing the age range.

During all this expansion there were smaller projects in both Madurai and Trivandrum that linked in with the home, the school and the drop-in centre. These projects were important but limited in scope through a lack of resources. There is no training manual for attempting to make an impression on the extremes of poverty in India. Large charities with skilled administrative backup were able to help on a much larger scale, but we did our best to show love to everyone we helped. I learned as I went along. The learning curve meant that some of the minor projects were more successful than others. My trust in some cases was abused but in others richly rewarded.

Chapter 18   Focusing on the Special Needs of Girls and Women

One area of concern to me is the low status of women in the Dalit community. A female child is considered a burden. Parents fear they will need to find a dowry for her—technically illegal, but still often expected. Then, after a marriage, the daughter will leave the parents and become part of her husband's family. Thus, she will no longer be able to contribute to the family budget or be around to help her parents in their old age. This is the context that helps to explain India's relatively high rate of female foeticide and infanticide. As the young girl grows up she will often receive less schooling than her brothers, because education is not seen as necessary to fulfil the duties of a wife and mother. She will then be required to marry her parents' choice of husband, a choice that might have been made soon after she was born. Many women find happiness in these marriages but many do not. At worst, they find themselves locked in a physically abusive relationship. On the other hand, staying unmarried can be worse. A woman without a husband, even a widow, has lower prestige and, with no one to support her and no marketable skills, she often has to resort to begging. Those who become pregnant outside marriage suffer even more.

In the Madurai area, many daughters of poor families stay at home unmarried, because their parents cannot afford a dowry. This is not a problem as long as the family can support them, but when the parents die, some girls end up on the streets. Girls who have converted to Christianity are often not able to marry because not only are they rejected by their Hindu relatives but also by potential Christian parents-in-law who doubt the sincerity of the conversion. I must stress that I am not making a blanket condemnation of arranged marriages. Jacob and Jessie's daughter Jemie's marriage was arranged by Jacob's sister, in accordance with their wishes because they wanted to ensure she would be cared for after they were unable to support her. As Jacob said to me at the time: "Who is going to look after her when we are not here?" At the time Jemie wept at the prospect of a marriage to someone she hardly knew. She was also upset that as a married woman she would not be able to complete her PhD. Fortunately, this marriage has worked out well. Jemie completed her doctorate and now works in pharmaceutical research in Bangalore. She and her husband and their wonderful little boy are happy and doing well.

Even among the higher castes, women do not enjoy the same status as men. I experienced this myself at the first board meeting with the charity on my initial visit in 1990. I was the only woman in attendance and the men did not know quite where to sit me. When the refreshments arrived, I was served last and rather reluctantly! One project which helps poorer women is to equip them with a sewing machine and teach them how to use it. Not only does the sewing machine become part of the girl's dowry, it demonstrates to a prospective husband that she has the tools and skills to earn money. In the early years in Trivandrum, we embarked on a pilot project. Mrs Abraham was a skilled embroidery worker and qualified teacher. She was enthusiastic about training unmarried girls to sew so that they would have a chance to support themselves. To begin with we purchased two sewing machines. The aim was to train six girls a year and we achieved this in the first year. Eventually, we set up in larger premises provided by the Lutheran Church, increased the number of machines to twelve and paid a teacher to train the girls. To help support the project, I brought the tablecloths and napkins they made in training back to the UK to sell at my regular presentations. Initially, we considered supplying renovated machines from the UK, but we found that we could buy new Singer treadle machines in India for less than the cost of refurbishment and carriage. Over one hundred machines have been purchased and double that number of girls have been trained.

In 2001, we developed the same idea in Madurai, with the formation of a tailoring unit for the women of the slum. It started in the drop-in centre but when that proved to be impractical, we moved to a hut in the slum. It cost £11 a month to rent and was big enough for five sewing machines and eight women. As the project developed we outgrew the hut and moved to two large rooms in a tenement building. Most of the goods the women made--shirts, tops and dresses--were sold locally. They also made clerical shirts which I was able to sell in the UK. The project was largely self-funding as the women were able to make a reasonable living and provide for their families. I have to admit I thoroughly enjoyed wandering round the bazaars to pick up material.

I tried to expand the production of clerical shirts for the UK but the only way to obtain an export licence was to pay bribes, which I have always refused to do. The other problem was that the women had difficulty in mastering the collar sizes, because in India the measurement taken is across the shoulders and not around the neck. Our first customers for those few shirts were the Bishops of Norwich, Thetford, and Lynn.

Another project that developed slowly but successfully was home sponsorship. I was able to arrange this through the Trust I had set up in the Trivandrum area. I became aware that there were often tightly knit family units in the slum and the rural jungle areas, who only needed financial assistance for the children to continue in full time education. A typical example was a widow whose husband had committed suicide because of their poverty. She and her elderly mother were trying to meet debts and keep her two daughters at school by rag-picking. We were able to help them by paying school fees, buying uniforms, and providing them with a box of supplementary food each month.

Another example is that of Anju who lived in a shack in a remote rural area with no toilet and no electricity. The shack consisted of one room, dark, damp and mosquito ridden. His father had died and his mother was sickly. We helped the family with food parcel supplements on a monthly basis and this enabled Anju to attend school.

Our help has extended to the installation of toilets in some homes or paying for structural building repairs in others. Home sponsorship needs careful monitoring as it is open to abuse. In order to prevent this, we visit the families every month. This prevents us from taking on too many families. There are hundreds who could benefit from the scheme, but that would be impossible for a small staff team to monitor.

Sanitation, or the lack of it, is a source of many debilitating diseases. Just outside Trivandrum, I began to have contact with the people of Vizhinjam, a small fishing village of about four and half thousand inhabitants. The term 'fishing village' is a misnomer as in reality it is a slum, albeit with marginally better housing and no open sewers. Drinking water is delivered twice daily to the slum but it costs two rupees a litre, a significant sum when the average weekly wage is thirty rupees. The people earn their livelihood from fishing. For the most part they sell the best of the catch and eat the waste fish themselves. The community is divided between Christians and Muslims, which creates some tension. We provided funds to the local Catholic Ladies League who arranged the installation of toilets in sixteen houses where there were teenage girls and no facilities at all. It is, of course, a fleabite in tackling an immense problem but we have made a difference in the lives we have touched.

It has always been an aim of mine to develop educational facilities beyond primary schooling. Our first effort was the Computer Centre in Madurai, which came about when a donor in Norwich sacrificed her holiday and donated the £2,000 she would have spent. This sum bought five computers, which provided our drop-in centre children with computer training for three hours each week with a qualified instructor.

The majority of children passing through our projects were living with at least one relative and our involvement with homeless children, particularly girls, was limited. But all that was to change through the television programme *Songs of Praise*. Just before Easter in 2002, the BBC decided to set one programme in Norwich Cathedral. They wrote to the hospital, where I was one of the Chaplains, to see if there was anyone they could interview who might be doing unusual work. I was recommended and, as a result, they interviewed me for the programme. I spent a whole day filming, during which I spoke and showed slides about the work in India to the presenter Pam Rhodes. Within a week of the broadcast, I received a call from the *Songs of Praise* production team to say they had received donations totalling £2,400.

All this coincided with my recent visit to Madurai when the police brought us five teenage girls, who had run away from home for varying reasons. They had raided the premises of a brothel agent just as the girls were about to be shipped off to North India for prostitution. As a temporary measure we accommodated them in the living quarters of the special needs children but this wasn't at all satisfactory. Our thinking was to rent a house and we soon decided on one that had become available near the new Centre. The £2,400 was enough funding to put a deposit down on the house and the interest on the balance enough to pay the rent. We employed a social worker and a housemother to look after the girls.

The housemother came to work for us through a rather unusual route. She was once married and had two children. Her husband died and shortly after his death she fell ill and ended on the streets. The police, probably for her own safety, put her into a brothel at the age of forty, where she stayed until some charity in the Mumbai area rescued her and gave her a train ticket to Madurai. Why she came to Madurai I don't know, but one of the workers found her in the Mellawassal slum. We offered her the position of housemother and she accepted. She proved to be wonderful.

Several people who sent us money initially continued to support the project. The aptly named *Songs of Praise House* is an illustration of how, when we have identified a need, we have been blessed with an answer to our prayers and found a way of obtaining the financing. About eighteen months after the original transmission, the BBC put together a programme called *The Best of Songs of Praise*. The producer contacted the BBC Delhi Office and arranged for a cameraman to film the House in action. Viewers were moved by the tree on which each girl had placed her photo together with details of what had happened to her. After the programme was broadcast we received a new influx of money.

By 2005, about one hundred runaway girls had passed through our hands. Some had run away following an argument with their parents; some had been ill-treated; and some had run away to escape early marriages because the parents could not afford to keep them at school. After visiting the family and checking it was safe for them, we encouraged them to return home whenever possible. If this was not a viable option we placed them with other institutions where they could get training and care.

The story of Vali is typical. After the death of her parents she was living on the streets when she was enticed into a brothel. Later she ran away. That was when the police found her and brought her to us. She was ten years old. She only knew the foulest language and screeched obscenities all the time. She believed men had only one reason for wanting to know her. It took two years of sedation and psychiatric work to get her to where she was quiet, calm and able to attend a special school. At thirteen, when I last saw her, she was happier but still traumatised by her past.

Songs of Praise was not the first TV programme to feature our work. Back in 1996 I was nominated for a 'Heart of Gold' award. This was a television programme where people were nominated, unbeknown to them, to receive an award for helping others. My involvement came about when one of our sponsors put my name forward. The BBC went to India and filmed the school without my knowledge. I was invited by the BBC to go along and talk about the charity I'd formed. I didn't realise until I got there that I would be talking on air with Esther Rantzen. It was an embarrassing experience as the project was presented in a rather sentimental way—but I was grateful because it brought in quite a bit of money.

By now I had been working in Madurai for several years, but this was to come to an end for a while. The charity that I had worked with to set up the existing projects now had guaranteed sources of income and could get by without the funds that I had been raising. So, I stepped back from Madurai for a few years and focused my energies on the developing Mavelikara project and the new post-tsunami work in Sri Lanka.

Chapter 19   Working in Medical Centres

Another area of our work that I've already touched upon is the medical work, particularly the efforts of the hospital and Dr Sindhu. As a result of that work I was contacted by the Regional Cancer Centre in Trivandrum, who asked me to set up a training programme for them. I found there a dedicated group with sincere concerns about the medical welfare of the poor. For some time I'd wanted to develop some form of medical facilities in the slums but the means and opportunity did not arise until early 2001 when we decided to finance a pilot scheme of annual medical camps.

The first was in the Madurai slum where, with helpers from Norwich, including two practice nurses from my own surgery in Brundall, we de-wormed five hundred children and cleaned infected wounds, ulcers, scabies, and sores from over a hundred people. It was hard and hot work. We repeated the exercise a few days later at Vizhinjam. Unfortunately, although this camp was a medical success things got a bit out of hand and it turned into a bun fight. A German charity worker, on hearing of the proposed camp, asked if he could attend to distribute clothes and toys at the same time and foolishly, we agreed. The result was that over two thousand people descended on the camp. It was blazing hot and trying to deal with the medical patients whilst others fought to get the clothes and toys created chaos.

The total cost for both camps was about £600 and hundreds of children and adults were treated and given medicines. We planned some follow-up smaller camps. Sadly, it was a drop in the ocean as most of the conditions would recur. The camps left me with the hope that one day we could set up permanent medical care facilities within the slums themselves. Always with me was the picture of a poor woman who walked two miles to the local hospital only to be given two antibiotic tablets for which she paid a day and a half's earnings. It saddened me to think how she'd been robbed, unaware that two antibiotic tablets would do nothing. We dabbled with the idea of an ambulance driving between the slums with two doctors who were prepared to give an hour or two a week but it wasn't really practical so it didn't go ahead.

And then in 2004 the impossible began to become a reality for the original slum.

A fundraising group from Brundall and Blofield, Norfolk was set up specifically to raise funds for such a medical project. The initial £4,000 to set it up was raised by them through an evening ball and 'Auction of Promises'. We envisaged a Primary Health Care Centre in the slum, which would occupy two rooms on the second floor of a tenement block. It was to be fitted out with some basic equipment and one of our girls Aniz, who had been with us all the way through and had just finished a year's basic nursing course, was to run it. In addition, three evenings a week, we planned to have a doctor and a community nurse, who would claim only their expenses. An important feature was the installation of a refrigerator to house antibiotics and rabies vaccines. In order to be effective, the rabies vaccine needs to be given as quickly as possible after a bite. Initial plans were to concentrate on immediate medical care, but looking to the future we would like to treat elderly diabetic patients who, without the means of paying for the necessary drugs, suffer and die very quickly.

An important part of our medical work today is with an Indian charity, *Care Plus* at the Regional Cancer Centre in Trivandrum. I first came into contact with the group about ten years ago, when I met Shoba its founder. *Care Plus* is a Christian charity, which provides counselling and medical and palliative care for poor cancer patients, many of whom are in the advanced and terminal stages of the disease. Shoba told me of an old lady who lay dying at the Cancer Centre. The prospect of cremation in the government morgue worried her, and yet she knew that her family would not have the money to transport her body home. So, in order to preserve the family honour, she hailed an auto rickshaw one day, gave the driver all that she had, and asked him to drive her until the money ran out. He did as she asked. A few days later her body was found on the roadside somewhere between the hospital and her home village. I was so moved by the story that we used some of our funds to buy an ambulance for the charity. This means that even the very poorest people can be assured of an honourable cremation or burial in their home village, and that those who are too sick or poor to travel by bus can be taken to the hospital for treatment or pain relief.

The acquisition of an ambulance has also enabled *Care Plus* to make home visits on a regular basis and to provide transport to one of their weekly clinics that are held in local churches. We also pay for the fuel costs, vehicle maintenance and the drivers' salaries. When the original ambulance wore out we replaced it with two smaller ones, thanks to some additional funding from a rotary club. The smaller ambulances are more practical and better able to negotiate the narrow streets where many of the patients live. Some streets are so narrow that the medical team ends up walking part of the way. Recently an ambulance got stuck in some rough ground in a remote country area and the medical team had to get out and push.

In addition to the medical treatment, the team does what it can to alleviate any worries the patient may have. The money for this part of the work comes from Indian donors and might be anything from getting a leaky roof repaired to paying for the children's education after the death of a parent. In one case, donors paid for an older daughter to have sewing lessons so she would have a way of supporting the family when her father died. Then there was the Muslim man with terminal cancer. When he became too ill to attend the clinic, the team visited him at home. He formed a particularly good relationship with a Doctor Philip. When he knew he was about to die, he asked to see 'his doctor'. The doctor on the team that week explained that Dr Philip could do no more than he could. "I know," said the man, "but I want to see **my** doctor before I die." The very fact that someone cares is therapeutic. As Shoba says, "A small helping hand can make sick people surprisingly happy." During the ten years we have worked with *Care Plus* thousands have been helped. I have been out on the ambulance on several occasions and seen the difference these dedicated volunteers are making in the lives of some of the very poorest people, many of whom are living not only with terminal cancer, but in terrible conditions. I am sometimes asked what Indian people are doing to help their own people; *Care Plus* is one shining example.

We have also set up two Palliative Care Study Days for the Hospital, attended by doctors and nurses from all over southern India. One was conducted by a sponsor Peter Speck, a well-known author and teacher of palliative care. A couple of years later one of my hospital colleagues, Pauline Greasley, and I ran a two day programme on spiritual and palliative care at our new complex in

Mavelikara. It was during the set-up of this medical work that we saw the first devastating images of the tsunami of December 2004.

Chapter 20   The Tsunami Creates New Needs

I was relaxing at home with my family on that Boxing Day when the dreadful news was broadcast. I made an urgent call to a colleague in Madurai to find out what was happening there. "We are unaffected," he assured me, "but a village not far away on the coast, has been destroyed. I'm sending a few of the older boys to help with the aid agencies but we could really do with you being here." I said I would see what I could do. Meanwhile I authorised £1,000 for food and water to be distributed where needed. A few days later I landed at Trivandrum airport. I wanted to get to Madurai so urgently that I decided I would drop a safety precaution that I had adhered to for the past ten years—I would travel there by road through the night.

To explain my fear of travel by night, I need to take a quick break from the narrative and make a few general comments about road traffic in India and the horrific experience I had in 1995. Travelling by road in India can be a terrifying experience at any time of day. The vehicles are often not roadworthy. I have lost count of the cars and busses I have ridden in with no tread on the tyres. Scant attention is paid to the rules of the road. Officially, people drive on the left but, due to poor road conditions, most drive in the centre. Vehicles swerve around each other, come out of side turnings without warning, and turn off the road without signalling. Drivers not only swerve around other cars and lorries without any reduction in speed but also around livestock (mainly cows), cyclists, auto-rickshaws and, in the absence of pavements, the crowds of people who pay no attention to approaching traffic. No wonder so many people die in horrific road accidents and travelling at night is particularly hazardous.

As I set out nervously from Trivandrum on the 4th January 2005, I relived the horror of the last time I had made this journey by road some ten years before. I was travelling with some colleagues and a driver who, once out of the city, gunned the accelerator and drove at a breakneck speed. The vehicle hugged the centre of the road with potholes every few yards, no cat's eyes, no white lines and no pavements. Cars were coming towards us head-on with headlights blazing. Our driver kept swerving and left the road three times. After two hours of this white-knuckle journey, I gasped to the man at the wheel, "I think we're going to have to stop. Is it like this all the time? How many are killed on this road?" His reply was terse. "A lot."

Then about 2 am we heard a tremendous bang just in front of our minibus, followed by awful screaming. A car had collided with a lorry, an open backed truck full of labourers had crashed into them, and then a mini bus carrying people on their way back from a wedding had gone under the lorry ripping off its roof as it did so.

Our driver swerved and we only narrowly missed being part of the carnage ourselves. There was diesel fuel spilling from the overturned lorry and terrible screaming from inside the wreckage of the cars. It was pitch black. I didn't really know where we were – but, despite my fellow travellers' insistence that I should stay in our vehicle, I went to help. Sensitivity for those reading this stops me from putting too much information about the horrific scene I discovered. A group of onlookers had gathered but no one was doing anything. The first casualty I saw was a boy, about eight years old, lying in the road. He had a severe head wound and was unconscious. I did mouth to mouth and chest compressions. All I had was a packet of wipes to clear away the blood. A baby lay dead outside the mini bus and, to my horror, a lady came over and tried to steal the gold chain from round its neck. I pushed her away. The boy had stopped breathing but with mouth-to-mouth resuscitation I got him breathing again. Because of the strong smell of fuel, I was terrified that everything would explode. While I was caring for the boy the same woman came back to rob the baby. This time I thumped her. At last someone came and started to pull people from the wreckage. The first two were dead babies followed by two young men, one dead and the other choking on his own blood. There was nothing I could do except put him in the recovery position. By now a lot of car headlights were lighting the scene; the carnage was unbelievable. The police eventually arrived but there was no sign of an ambulance. They commandeered a truck and threw the bodies and the boy I had been helping into the back. They told everyone to return to Trivandrum as the road was impassable. There seemed to be others trapped in the vehicles but the remaining police pushed me away. I stood helplessly

Slum children leaving the Mavelikara education centre after early morning tuition (page 137)

Girls from our residential home in Mavelikara

Early morning tuition

off to school

On most of my visits, 'old' boys and girls and their families come to see me—often making very long bus journeys

Muthukumar in the kitchen where ninety meals are cooked each day

Ladies at our residential centre where the love, medical care and good food they receive has transformed their lives

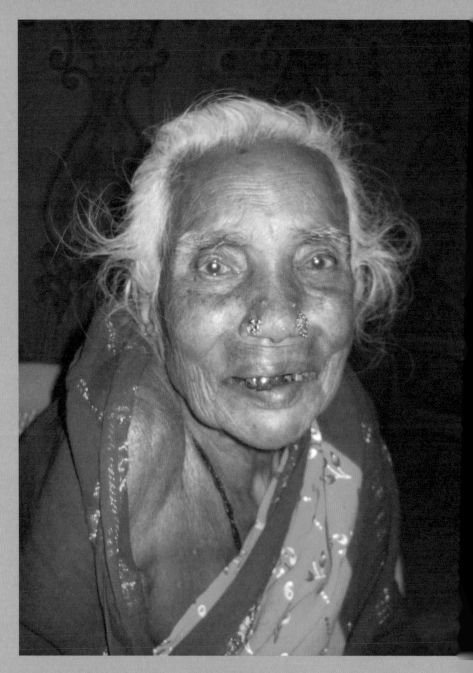

Alagammal, rescued from the streets, who said, "I am no longer alone" (page 141)

Mariammal, who spent a happy year in our residential home, before she died

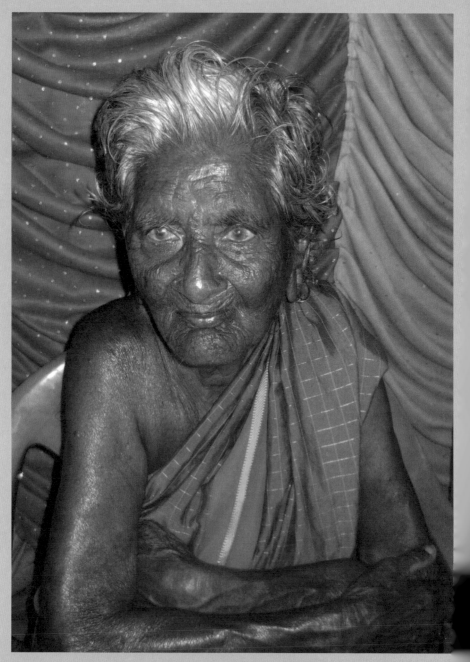

P.Karupayee, one of our drop-in-centre ladies who doesn't feel worthy to we
a blouse (page 17)

Elders from the drop-in-centre

This was a flowing river when I first started going to Madurai
(page 90)

Solaiammal, once a construction worker, says she is alive today because of the food and medicine she gets at the Centre (page 142)

Ranjith helps serve and Nagamma dances during day out at Father Leonard's (page 146)

Visiting the local guru (page 141)

Trip to the sea side
(page 143)

children from the Madurai project

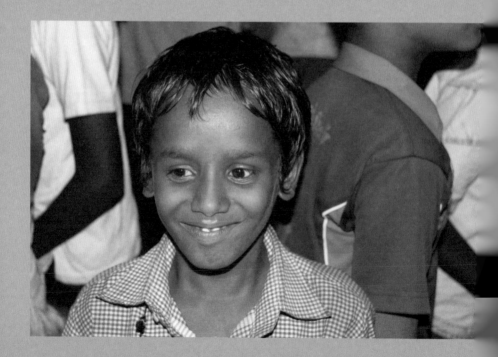

Enjoying a concert given by children at the drop-in-centre

Carole Blackwell with girls from the drop-in-centre

My family—without whose love and support over many years none
of my work in India would have been possible

watching them deal with the other casualties until the screaming stopped. I trembled and felt physically sick.

A family brought me water to wash myself. I had cut myself kneeling in the glass and had blood all over my hands and clothes. I could not believe that my companions had all stayed sitting in the van. They explained that people do not help at accidents in case they are held responsible for medical costs.

Our driver, ignoring the police order to return, drove through a field to get around the blockage and we continued in silence to Madurai. I went straight to bed and the dear housemother came in with sweet tea and a cuddle. One of the boys came and curled up on my lap and held me. I couldn't say anything, and the next day when I tried to speak, no words came out. For two days, I totally lost the power of speech. According to the newspapers eight people died in the accident, but I think it was more. It was also reported that an eight-year old boy had survived the accident after first aid by a foreigner. His parents and sister had been killed.

This accident, which happened in 1995, has haunted me ever since and certainly did on that January day in 2005. Fortunately, on this occasion we reached Madurai without incident.

The tsunami had hit a small town on the coast, where the main sources of income were fishing and rice growing. It was not a tourist area and life, already hard, had become even harder the previous year when a monsoon caused the sea to flood and contaminate the paddy fields. Then came the tsunami that destroyed everything. We set out to see for ourselves what we could do to help. As we approached the devastated area, we saw piles and piles of clothing along the roadside, placed there ready for distribution by the aid agencies. We drove to the offices of the Non-Governmental Organisation coordinating the relief effort to obtain the identity badges that would allow us through the police cordons to the beach area. The temperature was around thirty-eight degrees.

On arrival, we began walking along the main street. Where there had been the thatched shacks and brick buildings of a bustling community there was now a pile of rubble that continued as far as the eye could see. All around us were the minutiae of people's lives—a schoolbook here, a dress there, a broken figurine from a shrine, a cooking pot. Mixed among the debris were dead animals and human remains. An abiding memory is a shack about twelve feet by ten feet where two brick walls, though badly damaged, had somehow survived. In the ruin sat two women, one very old, the other probably in her twenties. They sat in absolute silence in a state of shock making no move to acknowledge our presence. The invasive stench of sewage thinly disguised by bleaching powder hung in the air. "Oh please God help them," I thought. "This is too much."

We moved away from the beach and spoke to some locals who said that at least three out of every family had been lost. Most of those who died had suffered severe head injuries from being slammed at speed against buildings and trees. Others had been sucked up by the receding water. I heard later the death toll in this one area was over twelve hundred. The main relief camp had been set up further inland but the people remaining were queuing at feeding stations, patiently waiting for sacks of grain and rice. As we walked towards the harbour, we passed several large boats which had smashed to pieces as they were hurled beyond the beach and onto the houses. In the harbour itself, boats were piled upon one another in a wild mismatch of colours. At the end of the street a connecting bridge was in pieces and the shacks around flattened. The army was working in this area. In the absence of the bridge, we waded thigh deep through water for about four hundred yards onto what had now become an island. Something bumped against one of my companions. It was a dismembered torso bloated from being so long in the water.

On the island we met up with two of the four older boys who had been sent from Madurai to help. They were distributing fresh drinking water from a tanker to a queue of people. Carrying water in any receptacle they could find, the people moved away and sat in the rubble, silent and numb with shock. Normally, everywhere you go in India there is noise, but here it was eerily quiet apart from the grinding murmur of the JCBs clearing the rubble in the distance. It was hard to know what to say to them. All I could do was reach out a hand and offer sympathy and a hug. A little boy came up and took hold of my hand as I was walking along the beach. He didn't say a word. It was very unusual. I stopped and spoke to him and gave him my pen. He bent down and touched my feet, a traditional gesture of humility and thanks.

None of us spoke as we made our way back to the car. There was nothing to say. Seeing such suffering made me, like many others, ask God, "Where were you? Why did you allow this?" I have no complete answers, but in the devastation I saw the love of God at work among the aid agencies. I thought of the suffering of Jesus and, as I looked around, I somehow felt that He was there alongside the suffering people.

Before we drove back to Madurai I left additional funds to be used for immediate relief, with the promise of more as needed. The next day we confirmed with the authorities that we would run camps and counselling for the children. We undertook to replace schoolbooks and uniforms. Until that day I thought I had seen the worst that India could throw at me but the horror of the tsunami was like nothing I had seen before. This was a catastrophe of Old Testament proportions. People had lost everything; homes, livelihoods, possessions, families and identities.

Six months later I revisited the area with some of our Indian helpers. Our major contribution was the creation of programmes for the children—many of whom had been orphaned. The camps offered lots of games and provided play materials such as skipping ropes, carom boards, chess sets, footballs, basketballs, nets, and badminton sets in an attempt to help them forget, for one brief moment. In collaboration with another charity we also produced five thousand copies of an excellent workbook for children, which we distributed with a pack of crayons, sharpeners and rubbers. Restoration work was proceeding slowly but there were signs of recovery. One elderly Indian woman said something that has stayed with me, "For once the world is united in compassion not war." So true, I thought, but for how long? The world moves on and we all so easily forget.

Chapter 21   Extending the Work to Sri Lanka

The emergency visit immediately after the tsunami preceded by a few days a scheduled visit of some of our sponsors, who had come to see the progress of our work in India. Amongst them was a valued friend. After the visit, on my way home to the UK, I stopped off in Sri Lanka as I had an errand to perform. My friend accompanied me. Two doctors from the Norfolk and Norwich Hospital had given me £298 with a specific request that it was to be used in the area of Sri Lanka seriously affected by the tsunami.

After putting our suitcases into a hotel near the airport, we wandered off in search of a local church that might make use of the money. The hotel had suggested a church about a half a mile down the road. It was Sunday mid-morning so I felt confident we would find it open. We were hot, dusty and tired and reached the church only to find it closed. We poked around the side of the building in the hope of finding the priest's house and came face to face with an unfriendly watchman who shook a cudgel at us. He ignored my attempts to explain who we were and chased us away.

Retracing our steps back to the hotel, I noticed a Don Bosco Centre just off the road and decided to try my luck there. The building looked derelict but as Don Bosco is a Catholic organisation set up to help street children I was quite hopeful. This time, I was confronted by a woman with a ferocious dog foaming at the mouth. Having previously experienced the sight of someone dying from a rabid dog bite, I didn't wait around but made a fast getaway and returned defeated to the hotel.

Later, I enquired again at reception, explaining about the money and that I was desperate to find a church somewhere in the next few hours. I was reluctant to put the money in some charity box without having any idea where it was going. "Oh," the receptionist said, "you ought to visit Father Terence."

"Who's he?"

"He's the parish priest of the Palangature District. He's the most wonderful man. Everyone here loves him. He lives with his people and a lot of his parish has been washed away in the tsunami." "He sounds just the man I want", I said. "Tell me where I can find him?" She explained his church was about a mile down the road in the opposite direction from the way I'd walked the day before.

We set off in an auto rickshaw but, on arrival, saw that this church, like the others, was closed. There were two beggars seeking shelter in the shade along the side of the church but the rickshaw driver refused to speak to them as they were Tamils. He was taken aback when I haltingly used the little Tamil I knew. I found out that the church opened at 3 pm. We had an hour to kill so it was back to the hotel for a drink before returning—only to find it still closed. We wandered around for almost half-an-hour and were about to give up when a man emerged from a hidden door at the rear. He was of average height and slender but he oozed charisma as he moved and spoke. "Father Terence?" I asked. He nodded and invited us into a little room inside the rear of the church. The lighting was poor and the room sparsely furnished with a few hard chairs around a bare table.

I explained that we were in transit on our way to England but had some funds to help people affected by the tsunami. He leaned forward gesturing excitedly with his hands. "I believe God has sent you," he said. "Several hundred of my parish members earn their living from fishing and many of the men have drowned in the tsunami. The boats they rent have been destroyed together with their homes. Two thousand are living as best they can in the open on the beach. The fortunate ones have tents." I asked how we could help and he told us that he had found a small piece of land where he would like to build one-room houses for his people.

He scraped back his chair and moved over to a cabinet. He pulled out a bundle of papers and spread them before us on the table. They were the plans of his proposed buildings together with all the receipt books of the money collected to date. I asked him how much more money he needed. "Too much," he said. "I'm £304 short." I took out the £298 in rupees and, without a word, handed it to him. Head down he slowly counted it. When he'd finished, he looked up at us and smiled. "You are angels sent by God."

Over refreshments, he talked about the suffering the tsunami had brought to his people. He said that a lot of the Government funds were being misused. One man who lost three boats had used the money he received from the Government to emigrate to America. There were others like him who had used the money to relocate instead of replacing their boats. With no boats to rent the people could not fish… He shrugged his shoulders and added, "…and without fish they cannot survive." He promised that any money we gave him would be channelled through the diocesan accounts.

We had no time to explore further his needs but, as a tentative first step, I decided we should finance the construction of two houses. This was but a pinprick to a people who Father Terence described as "the poorest of the poor". Among the people, the usual health problems of worm infestation, asthma, tuberculosis, and malnutrition were rife and the hand to mouth existence meant educating the children was a low priority. Many women had been widowed and to survive some were being seduced by the lure of easy money into drug peddling and prostitution. I stayed in regular contact with Father Terence and Sri Lanka became a regular stopping off point on my visits to Trivandrum. I set about finding sponsors in the UK for some of the children. We started with ten but numbers rose steadily to thirty-four. Sponsorship provided school uniforms, books and general financial assistance to the families.

Father Terence had given a lot of thought to the future of the sponsored children. For every sum given, he put aside £1-£2 per week per child. This meant that on leaving the project at sixteen, the children would receive a lump sum to help them set up a home or a small business. This scheme motivated the children to stay in school knowing that, if they dropped out early for any reason other than a family tragedy, the money would revert to the general fund. The idea was so successful that Jacob introduced it for some of our sponsored children in India. The Catholic diocese acted as overseer of the funding through a local committee of the villagers, with one villager taking responsibility for assessing the children, supplying the uniforms and materials and making sure they attended school.

In 2008, the HOPE team visited Sri Lanka and in ten days decorated the community centre Father Terence had built for his parishioners—an amazing job which included laying hundreds of tiles and a complete rewiring (no mean feat with the high ceilings). An amazing nine hundred plus children attended there for Sunday school. On subsequent visits I always found it spotless and well looked after. Father Terence used the local committee to ensure continuity in case he should move on. It was a wise decision, as he has now moved to Northern Sri Lanka where he felt drawn to help the people living in acute poverty and near starvation as a result of armed conflicts between government forces and the Tamil Tigers.

Our involvement in Sri Lanka worked well for some years but gradually it became harder for us to maintain the personal links we wanted to maintain with our thirty-four sponsors. These difficulties led us in due course to review our commitments. Over the years since the tsunami, family prosperity had been improving dramatically, tourism had picked up, and government funding had created more work. I discovered that the sponsorship money was no longer being used for food, uniforms and school materials, which was its original purpose, but was instead paying for extra tuition to help children catch up on the education they had missed. In Sri Lanka, as in India, higher education is the only way to break out of the cycle of poverty. If children do not pass each year's exam from standard one to ten, or if they start late or skip years, it is almost impossible to catch up.

I found that parents were choosing the expensive option of arranging extra tuition themselves, so we decided to implement a more cost effective scheme by using sponsorship funds to finance our own classes before and after school. Employing extra tuition teachers for a group of children rather than for individuals meant we could help more children. These changes gradually led us away from individual sponsorship to payment of an annual grant. In addition, the families concerned were monitored to make sure the children were being well cared for. Two friends of mine took on the sponsorship of girls who could not have finished their degree course without help. Both have now graduated.

Chapter 22   A New Beginning in Mavelikara

After making the necessary changes in Sri Lanka, we turned our attention to the work in Trivandrum. Sipping tea with Jacob and Jesse in their cramped office at the Trivandrum home one day, I could see Jacob was struggling to say something. He finally blurted it out. "Pat, my dear friend, I know you have much on your mind with Sri Lanka but we must do something about the conditions here." Moving to get comfortable in the tiny room I think I knew what Jacob was about to say. "We are running out of space and the buildings need much work."

I had to agree the buildings were looking tired. We had rented them from the beginning and stayed in the same area because the local church was supportive. It was obvious we needed more room and maybe now was the time to make the bold step of looking elsewhere for a more suitable base for expansion. "Are you thinking of the town where you grew up?" I asked. The Indian culture places great importance on retaining links with ones roots and Jacob, like most of his countrymen, had a great affection for his birthplace. This was Mavelikara—a small town of about 30,000 inhabitants not far away from where we were in Trivandrum and on the banks of the Achankoval River. As a result of this conversation, Jacob and Jesse arranged to take me on a visit.

My first impression on entering Mavelikara was of splendid churches and temples dotted between clusters of large concrete buildings and shacks, all set against a background of paddy fields and jungle. It was a backwater with never enough work for everyone. Conditions were bad with many workers earning less than £50 a year to feed their family—a family which could include grandparents, parents and children. Most of those who were not fishermen worked in the paddy fields. When the tsunami came it did not kill as many people as it did in other coastal areas, but it contaminated the fields with salt water.

lost of the inhabitants of this close-knit community are Dalits, with a fifty-fifty split in religious belief between Hinduism and Christianity. Although fifty percent of the children are Hindus, Jacob told me the parish priests were even-handed in their help to the community. It is common for both religious groups to celebrate Diwali, Easter and Christmas together. As Jacob showed me around, he pointed out that many of our existing children who weren't orphans came from in and around Mavelikara and that it would be better for them if the home were nearer their families. He said that the local churches had been in touch with him, urging him to come home. There were many poor children who were not well fed or receiving proper education and there was a desperate need for a school. Over the weeks we became more and more convinced that we needed to provide an environment for our children away from the city and nearer to their families—a place where they could run and play freely, and where we could also help scores of rural slum children. So we began to draw up plans. Ideas came tumbling out—a home for sixty children at least, tuition facilities, office facilities, workshops, and a large meeting hall with staff accommodation above.

Local clergy told us that they had all been praying for a school for the rural poor. Jacob knew of an acre of land at Mavelikara that had lain idle for years. It was adjacent to a paddy field he owned with his own house close by. We arranged a visit to view it and, as Jacob and I walked around the plot, I felt a calmness and peace. Beyond the dilapidated cowshed standing in the corner of the field I envisioned a brand new children's home with gardens around it. We went to talk to the landowner, knowing that land in the state of Kerala is expensive. Happily, after some negotiation, she agreed to sell it to us for £15,000. It was worth double that amount. Her only condition was that the land be always used for charitable purposes. Just what we wanted!

The purchase of the land went through smoothly and we registered it in the name of the existing Indian Trust with documentation drawn up by a registry agent and checked by an independent auditor. Having learnt by experience, I wanted to be sure everything was open and accountable and that the local people were fully aware of all that was happening. I very much wanted them to be involved. We then put the building out for tender. The trustees of the Indian Trust, well known to the local community, were to have overall responsibility for the land and buildings. The Trust deed contained a condition that if the Trust stopped functioning, or at the end of forty years, the land and buildings would go to the Church of South India. Registration took a great deal longer than I anticipated but the bureaucracy in India is always slow.

I grew more and more excited about the plans. They were ambitious. There were two blocks for the existing resident children from the home in Trivandrum and the capacity to double the numbers. Integral to each building would be school facilities. Although our children would probably attend local schools, we would build classrooms, a library and study facilities. The intention was not only to provide a home for our resident children but facilities that could be used by local children who would come for extra tuition. Oh, how the plans and ideas spun around in my head. I felt we had enough funds available to make the project viable but my enthusiasm was blunted when I realised the paperwork and building work would take at least eighteen months. "Can't we do it any faster?" I asked Jacob as we stood in the middle of the proposed building plot. We stood for a while, not saying a word. Suddenly, he pointed to the corner of the field. "What about the old cowshed over there?" he said. "It's out of the way of the building work. We could renovate it quickly and use it as a temporary school for some of the neediest local children until the new building is ready."

During the following eight months, we built a six-foot wall around the site for safety and security and extended and renovated the cowshed. Our temporary school/tuition centre was ready. Sixty-one children from the local slum area, who were having at most only a few hours education a week, registered to attend. Between our facility and the local church school, they were all soon in full-time education. Although we had limited facilities, we were able to provide breakfast followed by lessons. The children then went for a few lessons at the Church of South India School, returning to us for tea, snacks, more lessons and food before going home. We made use of Saturdays to provide extra tuition so those children behind in their education could catch up. The local churches recommended which children should attend.

We were blessed to be chosen as the focus of the 'Lent Appeal' of the Norwich Diocese that year and the generous donations that flowed in from the different parishes provided the funding we needed. Work was scheduled to begin on the boys' and girls' homes and education centres at the beginning of October 2007 and to be completed by the end of June 2008. These targets proved overly optimistic. Throughout it all, poor Jacob and Jesse, assisted by our Mavelikara trustees, were overseeing the new project while continuing to manage our current boys' and girls' homes in Trivandrum. All the children were excited and we reassured the older children that, even when they left to start work, they should still look on the new premises at Mavelikara as their home.

By early 2008, progress had slowed. It was clear the building work would not be finished on time: the footings were not yet in place and we were still trying to get the plans approved. This meant a rethink and a decision to move the children from Trivandrum in May, albeit only to temporary accommodation. There were two reasons for this plan. Firstly, Jacob and Jesse needed relief from the strain of commuting between Trivandrum and Mavelikara. Secondly, if the children were not registered in the Mavelikara schools in June, the beginning of the school year, they would have to wait another year. So the search for staff began. In addition to the teachers we needed house parents, two cooks and general domestic help for the new homes. Amidst all the upheaval it was thrilling to see the change in the local children. They were all severely malnourished when they came to us but at their regular check-ups we saw a marked improvement because of the good food they were now getting. There was no anaemia, no skin conditions and all had put on weight. One or two children needed major dental work and so we arranged for them to see a dentist.

By October the Mavelikara project finally cleared all the necessary hurdles for registration and building permission. So, after a year of frustration, particularly for Jacob who had to jump through all kinds of hoops to get us to this stage, we were finally ready to start. We had adapted our original plans to provide more room for play, and to make improvements in the gardens. The latter was thanks to a donation in memory of one of our sponsors. We looked forward to the time we would be caring for up to a hundred and fifty children on a daily basis. We rented temporary accommodation for the children in nearby homes, which meant they could see the building taking shape. A big bonus was that they had somewhere to relax and play as they adjusted to their new government schools. The pressure mounted to get the building work completed. Our school in the converted cowshed was full to overflowing, forcing one tuition class to use the veranda of the temporary girls' home.

The move to Mavelikara was not without its problems. Our girls' home in Trivandrum had a majority of senior girls who, having already reached higher education, would not be able to move away from their families. The result was that we reduced the number of girls in our care in the home to seven. We did not plan to increase this number (unless there was an urgent need) until we had the others safely installed in the new buildings. We provided the senior girls we left behind with college fees and maintenance grants for living at home and Jacob and Jesse continued to monitor their welfare. All have since reached A level standard and gone on to degree or vocational courses. There is no doubt that this would not have happened if they had not been nurtured by us in their formative years.

The boys' move was much easier as all but three of the resident boys transferred. Of these, two moved into vocational training in the Trivandrum area and one went on to study for a Master's Degree. Throughout the upheaval the school went from strength to strength. The children did not seem to mind the cramped conditions. In fact, it was rather cosy and there was a lovely sense of peace.

One day Jacob and I discussed how we could make use of the cowshed-cum-school facilities during the time when the children were away at the local church school. We both thought we could do something for the elderly ladies in the community who lived in really awful conditions. When Jacob took me around on that first visit to Mavelikara, we kept coming across these old ladies. Some, who had lost all their possessions in the tsunami, were living in small, dark, damp buildings erected by the government. Others were not so fortunate and had to make a home in whatever space they could find. Many were ill or partially blind from cataracts. Most spent their days sitting outside doing nothing.

As soon as we were operational we arranged for the old ladies to come each day after the children had left. Because we had a cook we were able to provide them with tea, snacks and lunch. The ladies spent the days resting, enjoying the gardens, watching television and chatting to one another in a loving and caring environment. In addition, we organised some basic medical care. For example, the common complaint of cataracts could be treated at a government hospital but the ladies had no transport. We had our original ambulance and with the voluntary help of one of our trustees, a nurse, we started to transport twenty ladies at a time for treatment. The ladies really appreciated what we were giving them. Their lives had been so hard. All had been paddy field workers, moving from shack to shack as they followed the harvesting in the fields. They had worked, as younger mothers still do, with their children strapped to their backs, only ever being paid in 'paddy' (the raw untreated rice). One of them once came up to me and hugged me and said, "Our lives have been hard but now God has given us love and care at the end of our days." Twice a year we gave each lady a new sari but one year they made a surprising request. We always made a point of giving each lady a sari that was different from the others, but now they were asking to be dressed the same. They had seen the children in their school uniforms and thought that if they were all dressed the same, people would know they 'belonged'.

Although progress was slow, by February 2009, work on the footings had begun. I watched stunned when I saw they were being dug by hand. Workers moved massive boulders on their heads. Women mixed cement and carried buckets of it to the footings, again on their heads. These labourers earned about £3.50 per day and, though we couldn't interfere with their wages, we did provide as much care and help on site for them as we could. The race was on to get the buildings up and the roofs on before the monsoons started in June. We completed all the final form filling and registered with local and state authorities and, most important to me, all with the support and encouragement of the local community who were on the journey with us. Everything was open and transparent.

As I watched, I dreamt of the day when the buildings would reverberate with the noise of children racing through the rooms and the humming of the working vocational units. Eight months later, in October 2009, Jacob drove me into the new complex. He made me cover my eyes until we came to a stop. He got out and walked round to help me out of the car. "You can open your eyes now, Pat," he said. Wow! Wow! And Wow again. The shells of the buildings were complete. It was all so much bigger than I had imagined. Of course, there was much more to do—decorating, and plumbing including the installation of the septic tanks. But looking at what we had already achieved, I had every confidence the building work would be completed well before the planning permission lapsed.

The grand opening was in February 2010. And what a wonderful day it was. We were surrounded by most of the children who had grown up with us over the past fourteen years and who had travelled long distances to be with us on that day. More than four hundred guests, some local, others from towns and villages throughout Southern India, came to see the new building. A highlight for me was the celebration lunch which was cooked by some of our ex-boys, who were now international chefs. They stayed up all night to ensure it was perfect. The Bishop of Central Kerala formally opened the school, the boys' and girls' homes, the granny centre and the dining block. I am not ashamed to say that I cried when a message of support from Bishop Graham of Norwich was read out.

What of the facilities themselves? They were, as I had dreamt, really splendid! Each child had the government prescribed eight square feet of bed space, and the bathroom facilities, showers and toilets more than met the criteria for the proposed numbers of children. Fans were fitted throughout. The floors were beautifully tiled and each of the residential buildings had a large hall area. The dining block was impressive and measured up to the standards of a high quality hotel. The Bishop said that the whole complex was a five-star facility! Outside were the beginnings of a play area and gardens. And we had achieved all this within a budget of £120,000.

The buildings are indeed impressive but that is not what the Mavelikara project is about. The home and centre is for children—around ninety of them from the local slum and thirty-one who live in the home. At 6 o'clock each morning they all come together for extra tuition and breakfast. Without the *iddli* (steamed rice cakes) and the chickpea curry or one of the other tasty dishes prepared by the cooks, many of the slum children would go to school hungry. At the end of the school day, they all return for more lessons. This extra tuition by qualified teachers gives the children a great advantage at school where individual help is impossible in the large classes. But life at the Mavelikara Centre is about more than school, food, and keeping the buildings spotless. Jacob and Jesse care for the children like kindly grandparents, supported by wonderful house parents and dedicated cooks. The children enjoy a variety of extra-curricular activities and are encouraged to develop their own particular talents. On a recent visit I enjoyed a concert which included action songs, acrobatics and dances. The finale was a 'kitchen band' in which dustpans, brooms, metal plates and chopping boards became musical instruments. Clever, original and fun, the dance was choreographed by one of the girls. Children who once were alone and unprotected, children who live in squalor and poverty in the slum are bright-eyed and full of hope. This is what the Mavelikara project is about.

Chapter 23   Return to Madurai: Muthukumar Joins the Team

While we had been concentrating on the work in Trivandrum and Mavelikara and the tsunami relief, we had not set up any new independent projects in Madurai. But I wanted to do this, since memories of the street children and the elderly ladies from the slums continued to haunt my thoughts. I could not forget the lined and hungry faces of the grannies. They were always in my prayers.

Then in 2008, I received an email from Muthukumar, the young man I had worked with in the past, telling me about a research project he was working on. I had a great respect for Muthukumar and was eager to read his report as it concerned the numbers and plight of the elderly on the streets and in the slums of Madurai. His call coincided with a recent article in *The Hindu*, a prominent Indian newspaper, condemning the fact that over 500 old people lived and worked on rubbish tips in Madurai, many without even a shack to go back to at night. I didn't want to lose contact with him again, so I asked him if, for an honorarium, he would research for me the effects of street living, particularly for the elderly. He did this for a year and I felt I had to return to Madurai to do something that would improve the quality of their lives.

After reading his well-researched findings on the desperate plight of street-living elders, my memories of Madurai came flooding back. We met and both agreed that urgent action was needed. We thought we could start by setting up a lunch centre, which would provide at least one meal a day. But where would the money come from?

The answer came one Saturday afternoon back in the UK when I was stuck in a traffic jam on the A47, on my way home from a fund raiser lunch in Cringleford. Since I was stationary, I picked up my mobile when it rang. It was the lunch organisers calling to say that they had raised about £4,000, twice as much as they had expected. It was an answer to prayer. We would now have enough money to set up a drop-in centre near one of the slums where elderly women could come daily for food, respite and medical attention. Muthukumar and I agreed to set up an Indian Trust in the Tamil Nadu State, to be used as a conduit for funds. I was careful to ensure the Trust was properly registered with an independent advocate and accountant to monitor the work. To ensure complete transparency we also identified some well-known members of the community, who agreed to become Trustees,

Until this point most of our work had been with children who had their whole future before them. Now I was also engaged in trying to help those at the end of their lives—old ladies who had a sense of hopelessness with only the prospect of a painful and ugly death ahead of them. The best we could do for them was to help them die with dignity, knowing that someone cared for them. We planned to set up the centre on the fringe of a slum which was home to over six hundred people. The slum had no electricity and one stand pipe that was only turned on for a few hours each week. There was one ladies' toilet that no one could afford to use. Our aim was to have the drop-in centre functioning by July 2009. This ambitious target was met, despite difficulties in finding suitable premises with the limited funds available.

The place we finally settled on was a small first floor set of rooms above a run-down shop. On my initial viewing I was sceptical as Muthukumar led me through a door to a flight of rickety stairs. "Are you sure these are safe?" I asked, envisaging landing bottom up through the ceiling of the shop below. He laughed. "Of course, Patamma." I was not convinced and tiptoed up the stairs sticking closely to the edge. The door at the top opened into a room about sixteen feet by nine feet, not much different in size to the average living room in the UK. It was dark, gloomy and depressing. Muthukumar could see my disappointment. "It will be fine, Pat. A good clean, a coat of paint and some furniture and it will feel like home. It is near to the slum and at present it is the best we can afford." Of course, he was right. It was the best we could afford, and I needn't have worried. The ladies moved in and were delighted. To them it was a rajah's palace.

The first ladies selected were identified by the police as those needing the most care. I was shocked to see how sick and frail they were. We have always dealt with desperately poor people in the slums but in helping these ladies it seemed our work had reached another level. After a few months we found that providing the facility of a drop-in centre as a place of respite during the day was not sufficient. The nineteen ladies we had gathered were so frail that it broke our hearts to return them to the streets or the slum each evening. One day Muthukumar looked at me and said: "Pat, we've got to allow these ladies to live in the centre permanently."

Once these words were uttered, the creation of residential facilities was a foregone conclusion and thus the centre became their permanent home. Initially we expected most of them to die fairly quickly, but we had not realised the difference that love, care, good food and security would make. When asked what the centre meant to her, Alagammal replied simply, "I am no longer alone." Above the door, we put the words: *Son, behold your mother*—a reference to Jesus' words to the disciple he loved. Although initially this was a low key project, I felt confident that we were starting something that was desperately needed. I pay tribute to the staff and volunteers whose immense work at the beginning was instrumental in getting the centre up and running, and who have created not an institution but a home. "My son," said one old lady, pointing at Muthukumar and smiling. At first, I intended to work from afar in an administrative role but that is not where I like to be. I want to be hands on, hugging and loving. I found myself more and more keen to visit and be involved.

It is to be expected that when a new project opens in the slums and surrounding areas there will be a great deal of suspicion about the motives of those involved. Not long after we started I received an invitation to meet the local guru which was a sign of acceptance and approval. Entering his shack I had to stoop low as the ceiling was not five feet high. The room was dark and oppressive and I could just see the man and his wife. They were considerably shorter than me but could barely stand up straight. They were a delightful couple who made me very welcome, and I knew from then on the project would have the full support of the community.

Before long, we were running three centres. In the main centre we had our nineteen resident ladies, with a further twelve or so who dropped in daily for lunch. The second and third centres were created on the edge of another slum nearby. Each day about fifty ladies came to enjoy a delicious lunch and a chance to chat, watch television and relax. All those attending were seriously malnourished and had major health problems, such as active leprosy, scurvy, severe cataracts, TB, and chest infections, all of which require long term medical attention. The second and third centres were (and still are) a couple of dismal shacks but the ladies thought they were wonderful. There was a lovely sense of community and joy at both centres and soon the ladies were healthier and sparkling in the new saris we gave them. Solaiammal was not exaggerating when she said, "I am alive because of the food and medicine at the centre."

It wasn't long before it occurred to us that the drop-in centres were underused. Before the ladies arrived in the morning and after they left in the afternoon, the centres were more or less empty. We turned our thoughts to the children of the slum and realised that we had a space where they could study before and after school. Most of them lived in small dark shacks with neither space nor light to do homework. The drop-in centres would be ideal places for them to study. We had been given the money to pay for tuition teachers in addition to providing basic medical care and much needed nutrition. The children's centres were run on the Mavelikara model. The children received extra tuition before school and breakfast. Most of them would otherwise have gone to school hungry or maybe not have gone to school at all. At school they received the free lunch provided for children throughout India. At the end of the afternoon they came back to us for more tuition, tea and snacks. We also provided a main meal for about twenty children who might otherwise have starved.

About eighty children came to the centres and we soon began to see changes in their physical health and well-being. By providing the food and space to study with dedicated teachers, we ensured that most if not all of the children would remain with their families and not become 'slumdogs', the word commonly used for children who run away to try and escape poverty.

Another initiative we developed was to get food to the few elders who were too sick to leave their shacks. Our staff also went out on the streets three times a week to distribute care packages containing multivitamins, a small amount of Ibuprofen, soap, a packet of biscuits, and other such items. All this extra work was made easier by the gift of an auto rickshaw which enabled us to transport food between the centres.

Another important part of our work with the children and the old ladies is taking them completely out of their environment once in a while. To me it is a sign to them that says, "You matter and you are worth this special treat." A two-day trip to the beach costs no more than £14 and a day at a water park £3. The first big trip we took with the ladies was a visit to the sea. It began with a train ride—a first for most of them. They were excited as they boarded and when they realised that they would each have their own bunk to sleep in they were overwhelmed. We stayed for a couple of days at the Church of India Youth Centre, and it wasn't until the third day that the ladies saw the sea for the first time. I was bubbling with excitement and got to the beach ahead of them so I could see their reactions. How can I describe the looks on their faces as they caught their first glimpse of the sea? Wonder? Amazement? Joy? For a few moments they stood transfixed and then a few of them ran to the sea and threw themselves into the waves, shrieking with delight. One by one the others joined them until only a handful remained on the beach, overawed, eyes transfixed on the crashing waves. For an hour or more forty sari-clad elderly ladies jumped and splashed and had the time of their lives. One lady couldn't take her eyes off the sea. "I knew it would be wonderful," she said, "but I never imagined it would be as wonderful as this". When it was time to go back to the bus, she walked backwards, wanting to savour every moment of this experience of a life time.

When we took the Madurai children to a water park, it was, for many of them, their first time in water. The excitement leading up to the trip was beyond their dreams and had filled the whole slum with joy. Most of the children were soon splashing and shouting excitedly, but one little girl preferred to watch. She sat dangling her legs in a water channel laughing at the antics of our very lively boys. Two days later there was an unseasonal rain storm in Madurai, a Godsend, for the people. The sewer channels filled with water and, for a short time, a depression in the ground became a lake. Our dear girl, who had been too timid to get in the water at the park, went to the lake to bathe. No one actually saw what happened, but sadly she fell into the deep water and drowned. We were devastated by the news and some of our staff went to visit the poor mother who had already lost her husband. Through her tears, she said that the one thing that sustained her was knowing that her daughter had enjoyed the happiest day of her life just before she died. The girl's sister attends our project and comes with us on our trips.

Things were running well in Madurai when, in December 2011, Muthukumar raised a new concern. I received an urgent international call from him at home in the UK telling me: "The landlord of the residential home wants us to move out…and I'm having difficulty finding more premises." This was serious. The Residential Home was the hub of the operation. Not only was it home to the residential ladies, it was where Meenakshi cooked ninety delicious meals each day. The problem was not the absence of suitable buildings but finding a landlord who was willing to let his premises as a home for street and slum dwellers. When I arrived in India at the end of January, we had only days before we had to get out. Muthukumar met me at the station in Madurai. Despite his best efforts he still had not found a place. I found it difficult to sleep those first few nights as I turned possible back-up plans over in my mind.

And then, the day before I left, I came down to breakfast to find a beaming Muthukumar and Rajendran waiting for me. At 9 o'clock the previous evening, Muthukumar had received a call from a landlord who said he might be willing to rent his house. At 7 o'clock the next morning, Muthukumar went to see him. By the time I arrived for breakfast a deal had been provisionally agreed and all that was needed was my stamp of approval. The rent was more than we had been paying, but, thanks to money raised by the Salvation Army in Norwich, this was not a problem. The new house was more suitable with much larger accommodation and all on the ground floor. No longer would the ladies have to climb that steep and awkward staircase. Another bonus was that it was closer to the slum and the drop-in centre. There was just one problem; it was further away from the part of the slum where several of the 'day' ladies lived. However, thanks to donations from two Rotary Clubs, we were able to buy an ambulance which provided a taxi for the ladies in addition to its main task of taking the elderly still on the streets to hospital.

Thinking ahead, we are now exploring ways in which we can use our own cows to provide milk for the children and to earn funds to help make our Madurai projects self-financing. The idea of doing this dates back several years when we began a pilot project of financing a few cows that were looked after by families in the slum. Unfortunately, this first scheme did not work out as we had hoped. On the visit that followed the start-up of this scheme, I was met by a worried Muthukumar. He explained that the people in the slums had enough trouble taking care of themselves and their families and could not give the cows the care they needed. The animals were suffering and needed to be moved to a more suitable environment as soon as possible. I spent a restless night wondering what to do with the cows and so I hadn't had the best of sleeps when I met Father Leonard the following morning.

Father Leonard is a Catholic Priest who, together with two nuns, had set up a charity for street children. Although we felt as though we knew each other quite well, this was actually our first meeting. The relationship had begun about eight months earlier when I unexpectedly received an email from him. His charity was the Mahila Vidiyal Trust and inexplicably two emails meant for me had gone to him. His initial instinct was to discard them, but for some reason he decided to send them on to me. His project could have been anywhere in India but it turned out that only forty miles separated his project from our own work in Madurai and we became email friends, sharing thoughts on vocation and ministry. We arranged to meet next time I came to Madurai.

There was a lot to talk about that morning and before long he was telling me about the homes and school he had built thanks to generous donations from a Dutch group. He said that when the work was completed he realised they had slightly over calculated the number of bricks needed, so he decided to build a cow shed with the remainder. With a rueful smile he said that the nuns were quite annoyed at what they considered a futile project. As they had neither cows nor the means to buy any, it would have been more sensible to have sold the bricks. I could hardly believe what I was hearing. "You have a cow shed and no cows?" Leonard nodded. "Well I happen to have five cows in need of a good home."

The relationship between our charities has continued. We now sponsor a few of Leonard's children and, earlier this year, we took our Madurai ladies for a day out to his home in the country. It was a school day but he had kept some of the children home. He had spoken to the children about making their guests feel welcome, but he couldn't have imagined how much the contact would mean to ladies and children alike. There was an instant bonding between the grannies and the children and many tear-filled eyes. The nuns had arranged getting-to-know you games and the ladies were thrilled by the concert put on by the children. After a delicious lunch, little groups of ladies and children relaxed and chatted together. One group of children listened avidly to a lady reciting poems she had made up. Another group rocked with laughter as one of the more extravert ladies 'proposed' to one of the young men. Some of the children began to dance and the old ladies looked on, smiling. Then suddenly, to everyone's surprise, Nagamma stepped in and joined the dancers. Gradually the children stepped back as the frail little lady danced on, seemingly oblivious to the young smiling faces around her.

So, three years after the return to Madurai, we provide daily tuition and activities for seventy slum children, we run a leprosy clinic, look after twenty residential ladies, and give daily lunches to another seventy. We have financed seventy cataract operations and provided basic medical care to over a hundred street dwellers. The work is unending and repetitive but that is how it is. The stream of the disadvantaged poor is like a spring that continually wells up and never runs dry. We can only take a bucket out at a time. For me it was wonderful to return to the city where I spent so many years as a raw and inexperienced rookie serving my apprenticeship. The problems never go away but they will not deter me from the work that I always knew I was meant to do. I find it heart-breaking to see the state of some of the street and slum elderly, but it is a joy to me that in some small way over the years I have been able, with the help of others, to do something about it.

Chapter 24   Where we are Now and Some Thoughts about the Future

Where to next in my work in India? With the passing years, I am looking to delegate more of the administration tasks to the wonderful people who work with me. I shall carry on with my visits with the main purpose now of consolidating the work in India already developed. I want to strengthen the structures already in place and thus ensure the work can continue without me. There are carefully administered joint Trusts in the UK and India with competent and willing volunteers and excellent managers at each of the main projects, with whom I have worked for many years. They will assume greater responsibility for the projects and leave me more time to spend back on the streets working one-on-one with the children and the elderly.

The building of the Centre in Mavelikara with a Boys' and Girls' Home and an Education Centre is now finished. The work in these units will expand so that children will leave not only with a good education but also with vocational skills. We provide for nearly 150 children, approximately thirty of whom live in the residential homes.

In 2012, we decided to utilise two of our spare rooms in Mavelikara as a commercial tailoring unit. As we have such a good rapport with local churches and the community, we will be able to attract enough work to make a profit; one that will expand with time to provide for the centre's longer term future. It is important to say that four fifths of the not inconsiderable set-up and initial running costs of this unit will be met by our Mavelikara trustees themselves—such is their desire to ensure our long-term future.

At the Regional Cancer Centre we continue to finance the running of two ambulances, which involves paying the salaries of a driver and a nurse on each vehicle plus fuel and maintenance costs. The ambulances have assisted between two and three thousand people too ill or too poor to get to hospital. We also have a sponsorship scheme that provides food to the family carers who are unable to work whilst looking after their terminally ill relatives. In addition, my chaplaincy and hospice teaching has enabled training in palliative care for hospital staff.

The work in Sri Lanka continues with the annual tuition grant.

Lastly, there is our expanding work in Madurai which is greatly assisted by over twenty volunteers. It is gratifying that many of this number are children we once picked up from the streets, who have now grown up; they are happy to give unstintingly of their time and are excellent role models for the children. The drop-in lunch centre provides food and medical care for over fifty elders each day and for many more on the streets. The residential home is thriving and we arrange cataract operations and treatment for tuberculosis and leprosy at regular medical clinics. On one of my recent visits I was talking to the ladies who had come for lunch when I noticed a frail little lady who must have arrived after the others sitting just inside the doorway. I found out that she was in the advanced stages of leprosy and had shuffled to the centre on her bottom. With some of our funds donated specifically for leprosy victims, we were able to buy a wheel chair for her and arrange for medical treatment.

The work with our young people is going well. Over seventy children benefit from supplementary teaching and nutritious food. In addition Muthukumar and dedicated volunteers provide dance, karate and roller skating lessons, a variety of workshops and numerous other fun activities.

We have an excellent relationship with people in the slum where we are based and we are now looking for ways to ensure that all our projects that serve them can be financially self-sustaining. After shelving different ideas as impractical, we have decided to buy land for a farm that would produce enough revenue to sustain our slum elders. Rural land is very cheap in the Madurai area and our advisors have told us that breeding cows and raising chickens would be profitable.

Another profitable scheme came to me while I was taking visitors to the slum which is home to most of our elders. It is a wretched place with no electricity or running water and only one toilet for six hundred inhabitants. All water comes from a stand pipe outside the slum, which is turned on for about four hours a week. One of our ladies told us that she pays the whole of her government pension to rent her rudimentary low-ceilinged hut of 54 square feet. The walls and floor are made from baked cow dung, the roof of thatched palms—a dark and dismal place. She told me that each time the government puts up the pension, the slum landlords put up the rents. And since only those with a registered address are entitled to a pension, over half of the elderly women we care for do not even qualify. Then came a Eureka moment! Why not help the women escape from this awful existence by building huts on our new land? We spoke to a local architect who told us that a 90 square foot hut, almost twice the size of a typical slum dwelling could be built for £900. If we built some homes like this, they would belong to the Trust and we could rent them to slum elders; that is to say, those who got a pension could pay a portion of it towards the rent. Partially paying their way would give the elders a sense of pride and would also provide some long term income for the Trust.

We have the money for the land and the cows so we plan to start fairly soon. When we find the right plot, the first priority will be to build a cow shed and a hut for a cow man. The milk we produce will be collected on a daily basis. Five cows should produce sixty litres a day for between seven and eight months of the year. We are aware that milk yields are smaller in the really hot months, but the hybrid cows we are considering adapt well to intense heat. It is innovative and a little risky because of the drought, but it has the potential to create a co-operative that could be a totally new model of self-help. We could provide the elders with surplus milk and eggs and they could grow vegetables fertilised by cow dung. The elders are excited at the prospect. Most of them grew up in a rural area and are looking forward to helping with the vegetables, cows and chickens. The search for land has begun, and hopefully during 2013 we should be ready to run. Our plan is to build between twenty and thirty huts, a permanent home for our residential ladies, and a farm big enough to support them. We will also need a gas exchange unit so that the cow dung can be utilised properly. Solar panels should provide enough electricity.

Ranjith, our newest staff member, who has just graduated with an MA in Rural Development Studies, will play a major role in setting this up. Wonderful to think that an impoverished seven-year-old boy we picked up from the streets all those years ago would ultimately help to secure the long term future of our Madurai project.

It's easy when talking of our work over the last twenty-two years to gauge success by glibly quoting impressive numbers. But to me statistics do not measure the everyday stories of people that our work has helped, sometimes in quite small ways, to lift them out of squalor and poverty. One recent event comes to mind. I was with Paula, a UK trustee, when we met an elderly lady in rags, making a living from selling dropped, often broken combs that she had picked up from the streets. She earned about 10p per day and somehow survived on this. Over the next two days we were able to get her to a bathing place to wash off years of grime, buy her a new sari and a box of sixty new combs. Now she could start to sell new combs and use the profit to buy more. We also gave her some money. The lovely end to this story is that a local business man came to ask what we were doing. He said that he felt ashamed. He and his neighbours had noticed the lady for some time and done nothing. He promised that they would now take care of her. A simple story. There are many more—too many to put in to this book.

The highlights for me will always be the children. I have seen so many of them move into higher education or take up jobs which, as young Dalit children, they couldn't even have dreamt of. I have been privileged to watch a whole generation growing up. One of my joys is seeing children who have left our homes return in later years to visit. Last New Year, almost a hundred of our 'graduate' children came with their families to join in the celebrations at the Mavelikara home. Later in the year, on an outing for our centre and home children, nineteen of our grown-up children, some with a new spouse, made a great effort to come and say "hello" to me. Many of them have overcome the prejudices that kept them in poverty and now hold down good jobs that enable them to raise their own families in circumstances so different from the ones that they grew up in. Success to me goes by so many names:

> Jacob-Thomas who grew up in our Boys' Home: now in his mid-thirties is married with a young son. He is a qualified carpenter and partly earns his living making wooden holding crosses for patients in UK hospitals. So far, he has made over two thousand.

Pradeepkumar who also grew up in the Boys' Home was the first of our many university graduates: he now flies to and from the Gulf setting up computer systems for his company.

Pramod, Selverraj and Vivekandon who completed apprenticeships as multi-cuisine chefs are now employed in first class restaurants and earning well.

Dhanya and Soumya, who completed computer courses to post – graduate standard, now work for companies in Trivandrum.

Lekshmy, who completed a course in textile design is now employed as a designer.

Remya and Dhanya are sisters whose schooling we sponsored. Remya has started an Engineering degree and Dhanya has completed a Diploma in Nursing.

Vijayakumar has recently completed his Master's degree.

It is comforting to know that their future families will not grow up in poverty. Yet it saddens me that although we have lifted hundreds more from the poverty of rag picking and other hardships of Dalit life, the number we have helped is but a grain of sand on the beach.

Here in the UK my fellow trustees Jo and Paula, stand by not just to help now but to secure our longer-term future. The innovative plans to create more self-sufficiency on our projects should start to take shape in the next year or so. I am proud to be able to say that we have throughout maintained our promise to send every penny donated directly to the work. Our very limited expenses are met from a portion of gift aid repayments and not from donated funds.

My life is India hasn't been easy but then God never promised it would be. There have been times of heartache and some deep wounds, but overriding all of these has been great happiness and lovely friends. I thank God for the blessings he has given me. And most of all I thank you, our supporters and sponsors. Without YOU none of this would have been possible. Your loyalty, financial support, friendship and prayers have kept it all going. This book is for you.

Chapter 25 Reflections on my Work and my Faith

It's now twenty-two years since that first visit to India and fifty two years from when I first felt the call to be a missionary. My faith has matured throughout that time. As a child it was mainly about loving the people, the music and the sheer majesty and wonder of worship in an Anglo-Catholic church. That early wonder will never leave me and I will always be an Anglo-Catholic at heart. However, from that childish beginning, my faith has gradually shifted to something less definable and more focussed on God. People are always curious for details of my conversion as if expecting a dramatic account of how God spoke to me from a burning bush. I had no such revelation because my conversion has been more of journey rather than a Damascene experience.

In the suffering of Jesus, I see God moving amongst the poor and the sick. I see God where the pain is. My faith is a thread that stretches back to that missionary talking about lepers and Jesus' compassion for them. He was prepared to go where they were, where no one else would go. The suffering He saw in his lifetime must be more than was written in the Gospels. I see Jesus in the gutter with the blind man, with the lame beggar, and with the leper. I can't divorce my faith in Him from the fact that, more than anything else, He wanted to be with those who suffered, the outcasts and the untouchables, and not with the Scribes and Pharisees in the Temple. It's that image of Jesus I carry in my heart and hold central to my faith. That's why India was inevitable for me.

I've never forgotten the words said to me by Archdeacon Dawson: "To work without prayer is presumption; to pray without work is hypocrisy." I probably lean too much on the work and not enough on the prayer, although prayer very much underpins the work I do. I was brought up on the ritual of prayer but prayer has a wider implication than that to me. I feel prayer is not just words but actions too. Putting my arms around an old lady who no-one has hugged for years is prayer, being with the children on the streets and making them laugh is prayer, removing maggots from a festering sore on an old man's leg is prayer. That is prayer and I know God is listening.

Mother Teresa used to say, "Every time you look at a child who is suffering on the streets you see the face of Christ." I know exactly what she meant; that's why I find Jesus more on the streets or in a hospital ward than in an organised worship service. When I look back through my life, I recognise how the suffering I went through has helped me to have an understanding of how people feel. I don't believe for one minute God gave me Stills disease and all the other sickness I endured but I do believe he's used it to heighten my senses and make me realise what people have to go through.

During one recent visit to India I returned to my hotel from shopping for something to eat. During the short walk back in the intense heat, I passed two homeless, scrawny old men huddled in a doorway. Then, an organised begging ring of kids dressed in rags besieged me for money. I left them all and entered my air-conditioned hotel room, lay on the soft bed, sat and sipped a cup of coffee and used modern technology to e-mail my family at home. At that moment, it hit me how stark the contrast was between their poverty and my relative luxury.

Like most people I've wondered why innocent ordinary people are treated so abysmally. Why are there untouchables? Why do people die in gutters? Why do people die from rabies in this modern age when there are vaccines to save them? Why do two million children die every year from malaria? Why? Why? Why? I've lived in it and seen it more than most Europeans and everyone says that surely it must damage my faith. Strangely, I can honestly say that it doesn't. If anything it strengthens it. The deprivation and misery is not God's fault. We live in a fallen world. He's given us free will and it's us who allow these awful things to happen. That's why I know if Jesus came back tomorrow, I wouldn't find Him in Buckingham Palace, or the White House, or the Houses of Parliament, or even in cathedrals and churches. I'd find Him in the slums. That's where my faith lies and where I need to be.

People often think it must require extraordinary gifts and courage to do what I do. How wrong they are. I'm not clever or brave. I come from an ordinary background—a woman with a husband, two daughters and grandchildren. I firmly believe though that God helped me, this ordinary woman, to achieve what I have. At first, I could not understand why my hopes of being a missionary were dashed because of my illness. Yet, in 1990, when the work in India started, I realised that many of the things that had happened to me and many of the jobs I had done over the years had prepared me for my work in India.

My life threatening illness and the subsequent struggle to find the courage to return to India also prepared me for the work. Of course, I am not saying that it was God's plan to make me ill—just that the deep reflections that followed those traumatic days led me to a greater dependence on God and a sharper focus as the work expanded beyond my wildest expectations. In short, my driving force comes from God and my sense that he wants me to take his love to some of the world's poorest people—a love that will bring some hope into their lives.

I don't 'preach' the Gospel. It's difficult to do that in India, but instead I do something I believe is more important. I try to show people the love of Jesus. Anyone can do it. You just need to go out and hug people. It doesn't have to be India. It can be where you live. It doesn't have to be children or the elderly. Everyone needs to be loved. In the UK, there are the homeless people on the streets sleeping in doorways, who've given up on life, seeking refuge in drugs and alcohol. Like the Dalits they are shunned and despised. But each one of them is someone's son or daughter; each one used to be a cute little toddler. Somewhere along the way the world defeated them.

I've never expected any reward for my work other than to see joy and laughter in the lives of the children and the old people. It came as a shock to me to be offered an MBE in the 2007 New Year's Honours. I went to receive it at Buckingham Palace with Brian, Jo and Claire, the three people who deserved to be there, because over the years they've made enormous sacrifices for me. And more than that, they've made them gladly.

I'm constantly challenged about leaving them at home, as though I would just go away and not give them another thought. I've never forgotten Claire when she had tonsillitis, ringing me when I was in India, sobbing on the phone saying, "I wish you were here." I've never liked leaving them but I think they understand why I have to do what I do. For them to be there at the Palace was important to me. On the day, we all dressed in our finery. I was petrified. It was a mixture of emotions swinging from terror to exhilaration. During the day we were separated and I was taken, a bundle of nerves, with others into a separate room to be shown how to meet the Queen, what to say and warned not to talk too much or for too long. At the investiture, it was two steps forward then bow, two steps back, bow, turn and walk out. I was comforted in my nervousness when I noticed a high ranking RAF officer ahead of me was shaking too.

It was an amazing moment standing before the Queen. She was so gracious, immediately putting me at ease. "You've obviously had to make a lot of sacrifices to do this." she said. "Is the street children situation as bad as people say?" I stammered my reply: "Yes it is. In fact, it's probably worse than most people realise. It's on-going. The gap between rich and poor is getting bigger." "You will carry on with the work, won't you?" she said. "I wish you well and thank you for doing it." It was a wonderful day for all of us.

Although the MBE was given to me because I was the one who made forty plus trips to India, in truth it was an award for all the people who've supported me. Another surprise, a little before the MBE, was a letter from the Bishop of Norwich asking me to become a Canon at Norwich Cathedral. The honour is bestowed on twelve people at any one time for long and consistent service. I accepted but always feel embarrassed about it because I know of people who have served long ministries and will never receive that honour.

It was a strange route to being a Canon as, despite being pressured by the Bishop, I'd always set my face against the priesthood. I saw my vocation as a deaconess committed to working for the poor and the sick. I never wanted to be a priest. I felt a deaconess was a servant of the church whereas a priest was a leader. Then something happened in the Mellawassal slum that changed my views. I was walking through it one day when I saw this little old lady, who lived on the edge of the sewer, shuffling towards a Hindu shrine. Her sari was almost in rags and she was bent double with some form of spinal deformity. I noticed she was clutching something tightly in her hand. The shrine was hideous, fronted by a dead cockerel's head on a stick swarming with flies. The old lady bowed her head at the shrine and opened her hand to show a number of red petals, which spread before her. I could see she was praying. I learnt later that she carried out this ritual every day. First, she would go the Temple and, as she couldn't afford flowers, with the little money she had she bought the fallen petals from the garland makers. Taking these to the shrine, she would scatter them and pray for her people. When I knew what she was doing a thunderbolt hit me. I felt a physical thumping in my chest. I realised that was what a priest was - someone who always wants to pray for their people.

It hit me so hard that when I came home I rang the Bishop, David Atkinson, who said, "Wonderful! I want to see you straight away." Six weeks later, I was ordained a priest in my own parish church. My hang-up was I'd been held back by my Anglo-Catholic background, where I saw the priest as being high up and the people being low down. That little old lady at that shrine made me realise it was really the other way round; the priest is at the bottom serving the people above. Accepting the honour of becoming a Canon has not in any way changed this view.

It was an honour that particularly delighted my mother. She and my father had both found their faith later in life. When I rang and told her, I don't think I'd ever known her so ecstatic. She saw it as the continuation of a family tradition started by my great uncle Hardwicke Drummond Rawnsley, who was a Canon of Carlisle Cathedral and co-founder of the National Trust. Sadly, she never witnessed the ceremony of my ordination at the Cathedral, as she died two weeks before.

The future? I am 65 as this book approaches publication, and 40 plus visits have taken their toll. And yet, during those years I have, in spite of heartaches and disappointments, formed special relationships that will ensure the longer-term future of the work and those we care for. I spend time now with young adults I have known since they were on the streets as little children—and sometimes with their wives, husbands and increasingly their own children. Now they are confident, intelligent and so lovely. Many are volunteers for our projects. The future looks bright and another generation is following.

Perhaps just 5 more years...... but while there is an old lady to hug, a child to cuddle and while I can support my wonderful friends, who knows!

Epilogue

It was a bright clean day. The dry yellow sand of the beach sparkled in the blazing sun. The tide was out, but in the distance white seahorses of foam flashed on the rolling surf.

Along the deserted beach walked a young man disillusioned with the world—a world of terrorism, corruption, genocide, AIDS, starvation, disease, drought and poverty. It all seemed so unchanging, so vast, that there was no end to it.

All was hopeless.

In the distance, he saw a figure and as he approached he realised it was a middle-aged woman. He could see her stoop, pick something up and throw it with all her strength towards the waves. Before it splashed into the water she stooped again to pick up another and then another and then another and so on without pausing for rest.

Intrigued, he walked a little faster and as he drew near, he saw at his feet, spread as far as the eye could see, hundreds of starfish, left high and dry by the tide. They were dying as they slowly dried out in the heat of the morning sun.

It was then he noticed what the woman was doing. She was picking up the starfish one by one and throwing them back into the sea.

To the young man the woman's actions seemed futile.

On reaching the woman, he asked her, "There are so many starfish, how can what you are doing possibly matter?"

Not pausing to look at him, she picked up another starfish.

"You're right. It can't matter to them all…"

With that, she drew back her arm and flung the starfish in her hand as far as she could. The young man watched it spin through the air until it fell into the cool welcoming waves of the sea.

She turned to the young man and smiled.

'...but you see,' she said, 'It matters to that one.'